Hooking
Rugs

Hooking Rugs
New materials, new techniques

Gloria E. Crouse

The Taunton Press

Cover photos: Insets, Rick Mastelli
Background, Roger Schreiber
Creme-de-la Creme (1985, 56 in. by 79 in.), hooked and sculpted wools, metal
elements. (Collection of Dr. and Mrs. Richard Harding, Olympia, Washington.)

Text photos, except where noted: Susan Kahn

TAUNTON
BOOKS & VIDEOS

...by fellow enthusiasts

© 1990 by The Taunton Press, Inc.
All rights reserved.

First printing: August 1990
Printed in the United States of America

A THREADS Book

Threads magazine® is a trademark of
The Taunton Press, Inc., registered in the
U.S. Patent and Trademark Office.

The Taunton Press
63 South Main Street
Box 5506
Newtown, CT 06740-5506

Library of Congress Cataloging-in-Publication Data

Crouse, Gloria E.
    Hooking Rugs / Gloria E. Crouse.
        p.   cm.
    "A Threads book" — T.p. verso.
    Includes bibliographical references.
    ISBN 0-942391-41-1 ; $19.95
    1. Rugs, hooked.   I. Title.
TT850.C76   1990
746.7'4 — dc20
                                                    90-10792
                                                    CIP

Contents

Introduction

Welcome Cats, c. 1855. (Photo courtesy of America Hurrah Antiques, New York City.)

Plunk me down in front of a frame, put a hooking needle in my hand, surround me with glorious yarns and I'm in heaven! I become totally enraptured with color, texture and materials. What is it that brings this creative spark to life in me?

Some call it rug hooking, but it's really much more than that. Though this work is based on traditional rug-hooking techniques, it has entered a new era. Actually, it shouldn't be called "hooking" at all. It's really a mix of many related techniques — hooking, sculpting, punching, tufting—all enhanced with odd additions of metal, plastic, paper or paints. I call my projects "hooked variations."

This book will lead you through the fun and creative possibilities of these hooked variations that I so enjoy. You'll see the results of the many experiments made by using just two basic hooking tools, the punch needle and the speed needle. Both are inexpensive and easy to master, and both offer endless textures and combinations not possible in any of the other fiber arts.

The very things that attracted me to this work years ago continue to fascinate me today—the unlimited use of countless materials and the

Nature themes were popular subjects in early hooked rugs like this one (1875-1910, 30½ in. by 35½ in.), which incorporates pine trees, holly, flowers and stars. (Photo courtesy of the Margaret Woodbury Strong Museum, Rochester, New York.)

absence of restrictions on the size or shape of the final piece. In spite of the tremendous selection of materials on the market today, it's still exciting to realize that you can make something out of the most common materials and have it become your masterpiece.

I've always had a passion for fiber, fabrics and textures. This interest probably started way back in childhood, when I carried around a piece of velvet instead of a "blankie." The interest expanded to include embroidery in grade school and sewing clothes in high school. This led to clothing design at the university and a continuing career in fashion design. All this proved to be a good background, but not at all the creative career of which I had dreamed. At the time I discovered rug hooking, I was seeking a diversion — something different, fun and relaxing to do in fiber that required minimal equipment and training. Knitting and needlepoint didn't seem right; weaving was too complicated and costly. I remembered what fun I had had as a child, playing with my grandmother's shuttle hook and all those wonderful yarns that I wasn't supposed to touch. In my search for that old hook, I found the only hook in town — the punch needle I still love and use today.

As I remember, this tool cost only around $5 back then and came without instructions, not even pictures. As it turned out, the lack of instructions was probably the best thing that could have happened to me. It forced me to try everything to see just how versatile this needle could be. I'm sure I would never have tried all those unusual materials with that first hook if I'd had a teacher watching over me. What started innocently as a pastime soon became a full-time addiction. I gave up fashion design to spend more and more time with a hook in my hand.

Since then, I've tried every hooking tool I can get my hands on, new and antique. Dozens of hooks have evolved over the years, each making the basic loops with different mechanisms and many that are able to adjust the loop length. Each hook offers its own little pleasures not possible with another, but most are very restrictive with regard to the size and type of yarns and materials that they can easily accommodate. Of the many hooks I've tried, I find that the two basic ones — my original punch needle and the more recent speed needle — can accomplish everything I need or want to create. And they can handle an enormous variety of materials and techniques with ease and speed.

The traditional rug-hooking tool resembles a crochet hook set in a wooden handle, and it's still popular and available today. This traditional tool is inserted into the right side of the backing material and pulls loops of yarn or fabric strips from the wrong side of the backing to the right side. The length of the loop is determined by how far the yarn or fabric strip is pulled above the surface of the backing. Although working with this tool is slower than with other hooking needles, it has the advantage of allowing you to work from the right side. Most other hooks require working on the wrong side of the canvas.

Many modern hooks are referred to as "speed hooks," which gives a misleading impression that they are uncontrollable. (In fact, they all work just one loop at a time and do so only as fast as you wish.) There are, however, several electric needles on the market that are truly "speed" needles. Most are used for commercial hooking or production work, and these are best suited for less precise or controlled techniques.

In spite of the many different hooks and the newer technology, all these techniques originated in the early craft of rug hooking, considered to be one of America's few indigenous folk arts. History indicates that rug hooking probably began on or near the Maine coast in the 1840s and later spread to rural areas of New England and Pennsylvania. It's interesting to note that earlier rugs were not made for the floor — Colonial homes had bare floors — but as coverlets for beds. Colonial possessions were treasured, the bed most of all. These handmade sewn works, created for warmth and decoration, were known as bed-ruggs, and gave rise to the expression, "snug as a bug in a rug."

In the early decades of the 1800s, shirred and yarn-sewn hearth rugs were made to cover and protect more expensive manufactured rugs from fireplace ash and sparks. As the domestic textile industry developed in the United States, "store-bought" yardage and leftover scraps of clothing became ready sources of material for rugs. Hooked rugs developed both as an alternative to more expensive manufactured rugs and as an outlet for individual expression. The backing foundation was often handwoven linen or used burlap sacks from food provisions. Cloth strips were pulled up through the surface with a bent piece of metal, a nail or a carved piece of wood or bone.

Rug hooking flourished through the end of the 19th century. It was still considered a rural craft, and the designs reflected everyday country life, with frequent use of floral patterns, houses and farmyard animals. Motifs representing patriotic sentiment were another favorite theme. Later, patterns and kits were offered through the two major mail-order firms of the time, Sears, Roebuck and Montgomery Ward. Rug-hooking popularity dwindled, however, in the early 20th century, when, with increasing industrialization, it became more fashionable to have factory-made floor coverings.

In the northeastern United States and Canada, rug hooking developed into a cottage industry, with many rural communities centered around the handicraft. In the 1920s, a revival of interest in early American work spurred renewed interest in the craft. Shortly afterwards, traditional rug hooking found a champion in Pearl Kinnear McGown of Clinton, Massachusetts, an energetic teacher and writer whose books, classes, correspondence courses and rug patterns reached an ever-widening circle of hooking enthusiasts.

Aside from the traditionalists who had followed the craft of rug hooking through the decades, very few innovative artists took advantage of the new technologies in hooking tools to bring this fiber medium up to the contemporary level enjoyed by most other crafts. One exception was George Wells, of Long Island, New York, who was a major influence on rug hooking in the 1940s and 1950s. Wells died in 1988, but his influence is still felt throughout the country for his inspirational use of the punch needle. His business is still in operation, one of the few offering rug-hooking supplies (see Resources on p. 143).

The lack of development in contemporary hooking becomes more pronounced in light of the history of other crafts. After World War II, there was a craft renaissance in the United States, and artists began experimenting with traditional craft media, pushing them to new levels. A new aesthetic emerged, supported in part by the increased educational opportunities at universities, colleges and independent seminars and workshops. In the fiber arts, weaving, in particular—with its expensive looms and equipment—began to flourish, and yarns, materials and classes were readily available. Not

This long hearth rug (1850-1860, 16 in. by 91 in.) is quite rare, but the rural motifs are those found in many hooked rugs of the era. Its cotton pile is hooked on a brown hemp ground. According to oral history, the rug was made in Pennsylvania. (Photo courtesy of Allentown Art Museum, Allentown, Pennsylvania.)

Yellow House, c. 1920. (Photo courtesy of America Hurrah Antiques, New York City.)

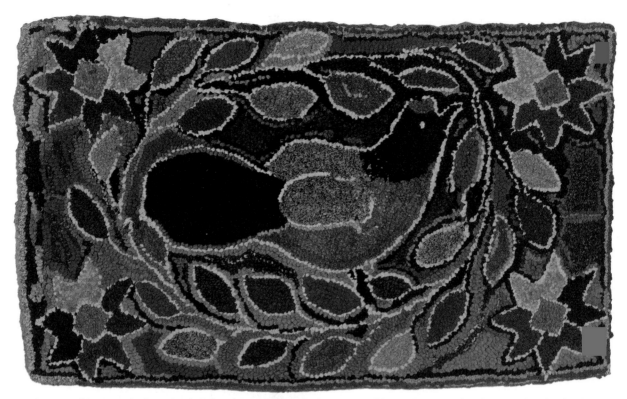

A cheery robin was the inspiration for this original design created by a New England rugmaker in the late 19th century. The work (18 in. by 31 in.) was hooked in wool fabric strips on a hemp backing. (Photo courtesy of Allentown Art Museum, Allentown, Pennsylvania.)

so with hooking, which remained a simple craft with simple tools. Even today, it can still prove difficult at times to locate and purchase hooking equipment — and even more challenging to find anyone teaching or inspiring the craft in new directions.

Fortunately, the needs for hooking are basic, and the individuals pushing the creative limits of the field are growing in number every day. Recently, fiber artists, along with painters and even architects, have discovered a new space for their individual artistic statements — the floor. I credit Rebeccah A. T. Stevens of The Textile Museum in Washington, D. C., with being the first person to recognize the lack of exhibitions of contemporary rugs in either galleries or museums. She was curator of the exhibition *Country of Origin, USA: A Decade of Contemporary Rugs* in 1984, which gave hooked rugs a new visibility in the field of decorative arts. The exhibit was well received, not only in the United States but also throughout South America, where it had an extended tour.

Shortly thereafter, the prestigious American Craft Museum in New York City staged their *For The Floor* exhibition, an international invitational that toured the United States for a year. Since then, we have had contemporary rugs shown throughout the United States, and the trend has followed in Japan and Europe. We also see more and more galleries featuring hooked rugs and growing interest from interior designers and their clients who enjoy art for the floor.

It's encouraging to witness this revival in rug hooking. What a delight, too, to find those wonderful hooked rugs of the past now being featured in leading national publications. Antique rugs are finding their way into major auction houses, commanding very high prices, as collectors realize their value as creative examples of times past.

The beauty of tradition continues in rug hooking, passed from generation to generation, as individuals create patterns and motifs in standard stitches. Following a parallel but distinctly different path, the contemporary rug-hooking artist risks the unknown, inventing and exploring new possibilities. It takes a gust of inspiration and a heck of a lot of courage to create, but if ever a natural creative environment was possible, it's with these hooked variations. With so much material so easily available, we have all the ingredients to stretch our abilities to the limit. You don't have to be gifted or brilliant to make some wonderful rugs — just suppress your fear and jump in.

I hope this book will reinforce your individual abilities and extend your talents to include this exhilarating craft. Remember, anyone can make a rug. And everyone should.

Simple Simon (c. 1930, 24 in. by 36 in.), by an unknown maker, was hooked in wool on burlap. (From the collection of the Museum of American Folk Art, New York City; gift of Mrs. Marilyn French).

1

Getting Started

r ug hooking took me by surprise more than 25 years ago. Once I began my first rug, I was hooked for good. Even though the techniques and materials of rug hooking have been around for at least 150 years, I was astonished to find how expressive and contemporary this craft could be. I quickly become enamored with the simplicity of the process and the rich textures the materials could yield. Over the years, rug hooking has never failed to stir my imagination or fill my mind with creative possibilities.

One of the biggest advantages in starting this fiber work is that it can be very simple and inexpensive. One hooking needle, a few yarns or fabrics, a wood frame and scissors—and you're set! You don't have to be gifted. You just need to have a mad desire to create your own masterpiece.

The biggest disadvantage to this work is that it becomes so infectious that you start collecting everything under the sun. And what's worse, it's never enough. You'll start looking at all materials differently. Will it go through the needle? How will it look in a high loop? Or when sculpted? What about dyed, painted or cut? Whenever I come across new materials—and few escape my eyes—my mind races with possibilities.

The remarkable thing about this craft is that you can hook almost anything if it will fit through the hooking needle. Yarns have been a traditional choice, but other materials like cut yardage can yield wonderful textures. Novelty yarns, metallics, plastics and even light-gauge wire can create unique effects in your work. The only limit is your imagination.

The sources of fabric are endless: sewing remnants, clothing, new yardage, blankets, sheets and other linens. I never include worn materials, since I want the finished work to last forever, but some rug hookers are doing nice things with faded denims (be sure to wash any worn fabrics before cutting the yardage or hooking). With a background in sewing, I started with a good supply of remnants. But you don't have to wait until you have a warehouse full. You can begin with just a skein of yarn. Get the feel of the hooking tool and try one yarn to see the many textures it can produce and the different possibilities it offers. You'll be surprised to find you can master the basic techniques in an afternoon, and the excitement of all the glorious textures will suggest enough ideas of what to collect to keep you busy for a long time.

When I look at my studio, my basement and garage—all overflowing with wonderful materials—I feel a little hesitant to encourage others to follow my addictive ways. But the following suggestions may help you begin to think about what to collect and where you might find it. When you come upon a new material that has rug-hooking possibilities, ask yourself some simple questions:

- Does it excite me? That's the primary criterion. Unless materials affect you emotionally, they should be passed by, because if you are not interested in the material, your finished work will show that lack of interest. But if a material captures your attention, then consider some other important points.

- How can I use it? Half of the time I can't answer this question. But I do know that if it excites me and seems to have a great hidden potential, I'll put it to good use.

- Can I afford it? If the material really grabs me emotionally and I feel I can't live without it, I buy it regardless of price. Most of the time, however, I'm quite sensible and mentally calculate how much I need versus how much I'm willing to spend. I look to see if the potential of the material warrants the price. Can I achieve a similar effect with another, less expensive choice? If so, I will probably pass it by.

- What quantity is available? This is a point often overlooked when purchasing materials. Is this one available only now, or if my project doesn't get completed immediately, will it be available next year? If this is a one-time offer, I frequently have a problem calculating how much to buy. So I just guess, depending upon the cost. If it's a fantastic buy, I hoard.

Selecting materials always involves a combination of decisions—color, texture, cost, availability, quantity and quality. I try to keep an open mind about materials, and I've learned that an enormous variety of fibers and materials can be used for hooking rugs. In the end, the decision about what materials to select always entails a balance of needs, budget and desired results. For example, wonderfully sensuous yarns and fabrics are hard to resist, but their desirability is usually matched by a steep price tag. I try to use control and good judgment, because I know that great textures can be made just as easily from simple materials as from expensive yarns.

Bargains, however, are my undoing. I cannot resist sales, mill ends, remnant stacks, garage sales, salvage yards, mail order and all points between. The best bargains are materials for free, and I suggest you never turn down a thing. Once people know you put all this "ridiculous stuff" to good use, they will bombard you with everything. Friends love to help, and they enjoy seeing the results. I've even gone to exhibition previews of my work and heard someone exclaim, "There's my daughter's high-school dress!" Friends who sew are especially good resources. It's not unusual for me to come home and discover a bag of sewing

A wide variety of materials can be used in rug hooking, from yarns and cut fabric strips to plastics and metal wire. The possibilities are as unlimited as your imagination.

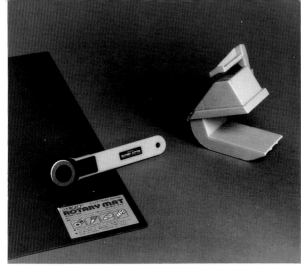

Cloth strippers are used to cut yardage into uniform strips for hooking. Seen above are the hand-held Olfa cutter and a self-healing cutting mat (left) and the Strip-It (right).

The Rigby cutter, at right, uses a series of interchangeable cutting wheels to create precise strips from ⅛ in. to ¼ in. wide. With a simple turn of the crank, as shown below, the Rigby turns flat yardage into multiple strips of fabric ready to be hooked.

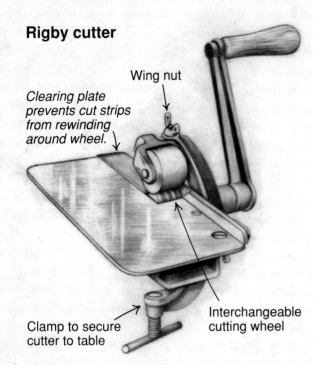

Rigby cutter

Clearing plate prevents cut strips from rewinding around wheel.

Wing nut

Interchangeable cutting wheel

Clamp to secure cutter to table

Preparing fabric for hooking

Materials used in rug hooking must be able to pass through the small eye of the hooking needle. Some materials, like yarns, can be used just as they are. Others, like fabric yardage and remnants, need to be cut into narrow strips and prepared before they can be hooked. Cloth strips produce hooked textures and surfaces unlike those made with plain or novelty yarn. What's most exciting with cut cloth is that the finished hooked strips often look entirely different from the flat yardage. Once you've started working with cloth strips, the creative possibilities will leap out at you.

Cutting cloth strips

Various tools are available for cutting fabric into strips, ranging from a basic pair of scissors to tools specifically designed for this purpose. Cloth cutters (also known as cloth strippers) enable you to cut multiple strips of fabric at the same time. The three cutters I use most often are the Rigby cutter, the Olfa cutter and the Strip-It.

As of this writing, the Ribgy costs $75, with additional cutting wheels priced at $10. The Olfa cutter is $10, plus from $5 to $30 (depending on size) for a self-healing cutting mat. The Strip-It costs $10. These tools are most easily bought by mail order (see pp. 141-143 for the addresses of some suppliers); prices are approximate and do not include shipping charges.

The Rigby cutter is a jewel and a necessity for anyone with a quantity of yardage, remnants or garments to cut. As you can see from the photos of my work throughout this book, it's rare that I don't combine cut cloth with yarns. Without the Rigby, I'm certain my work would have taken a completely different direction.

The Rigby (see the drawing above left) clamps on a table edge and operates by passing fabric between a set of interchangeable cutting wheels and a metal plate. The cutting wheels each have three or four blades, which make precision cuts from ⅛ in. to ¼ in. wide. With the simple turn of a crank handle, the Rigby cuts three to four adjacent strips of cloth of exactly the same width. The length of

remnants outside my door. After all the years of collecting, I still feel like a kid at Christmas going through a bag of fiber goodies.

Locating sources of supplies is always a difficult task for fiber workers. There is no single source, and about the time you discover ones that can serve you, they go out of business or cannot get what you just decided you can't live without. Most of the time you'll do best by mail order, for both variety and good prices. The best sources of information for these are the advertisements in the fiber, craft and art magazines (see Resources on pp. 143-145). You may have to spend a few dollars for sample swatches or a catalog, but it's well worth it. Since I work full time and on a large scale, I do most of my purchasing by mail. Any local yarn/weaving shop is a natural first place to shop for those just beginning rug hooking.

Sometimes hard-to-find materials, such as the right metallic fibers, wire or novelty goods, can be in short supply. When I see some I especially like, I buy them, knowing I may not find them when I need them. If a material has an unlimited availability, I refrain from buying it until I need it. But I commit the source information to memory, so I won't be frustrated later when I need to locate it.

the strip is determined by the length of the fabric passed through the cutter.

Over the past 25 years, I've used just three cutting wheels for my Rigby: #6, which cuts strips ³⁄₁₆ in. wide; #7, which cuts strips ⁷⁄₃₂ in. wide; and #8, which cuts strips ¼ in. wide. The cutting wheels are interchangeable and easily changed. Once the blade is in place, the wing nut on top is tightened just enough to create the correct tension for cutting through the cloth. I do this cautiously, turning in ⅛-in. increments so as to cut only the cloth but not the surface underneath, which would dull the blade. To date, I've never needed to resharpen any blades.

After the Rigby, the Olfa cutter, shown in the drawing below, is probably the next best tool for cutting cloth. I've only recently been introduced to the Olfa and haven't had a lot of experience with it, but because it's inexpensive, I encourage others to try it if they're dubious about investing in the Rigby. The Olfa cutter is a small hand tool with a rotating wheel that can cut through up to nearly ½ in. of layered cloth at one time. Because the circular blade is extremely sharp, the purchase of a self-healing cutting mat is recommended to pro-tect both the blade and the cutting surface (replacement blades are available).

The Olfa can cut strips of any width. Narrow widths like the ¼-in. strips commonly used in hooking are more difficult to cut than wider strips, but using a metal ruler or straightedge as a cutting guide helps keep the rolling cutter advancing in a straight line. Accuracy and precision depend on the skill of the operator. The Olfa is a good cutting tool, but I wouldn't like to rely on it for cutting all the yardage for a large project.

The third cloth stripper I commonly use is the Strip-It, a plastic device with four razor-type blades, which clamps on a table. Fabric is cut by holding the yardage taut and pulling it through the cutter from back to front. The Strip-It's removable blades are set into ¼-in. slots in the cutter, offering different options for cutting width. With all blades in place, four ¼-in. strips can be cut at once. By removing some of the blades, widths ranging from ½ in. to 1 in. can be cut.

The Strip-It is an inexpensive alternative to the Rigby, and, unlike that tool, will cut leather. The disadvantages of the Strip-It are that it cuts widths only between ¼ in. and 1 in. and that it cuts only on the straight grain. The Strip-It works best on sturdy materials with a firm weave. Fragile materials cannot hold up to the tension needed to pull the yardage through the cutting blades. Also, I've not been able to find replacement blades for the Strip-It, which means that you may need to buy a whole new unit when the blades become too dull.

If you don't have a cutter, you can tear fabric into strips or cut it by hand with a pair of scissors. These methods work best for cutting small amounts of strips, however, and I would never recommend cutting by hand for a large project. I remember cutting strips by hand for one of my earliest projects, a 4-ft. by 6-ft. rug that combined wool yarns with wool strips from coats, remnants, yardage and even a new blanket. From that experience, I decided that I would never again cut all those strips by hand; I also learned that it takes a tremendous amount of cloth to hook a project that size. I was so caught up in the excitement of my first large-scale project that I couldn't slow down. But after nursing countless blistered fingers, I mailed my order for a cloth stripper, which has since done all my cloth stripping for me.

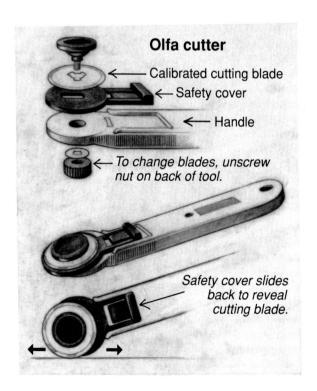

Olfa cutter

← Calibrated cutting blade

← Safety cover

← Handle

← *To change blades, unscrew nut on back of tool.*

Safety cover slides back to reveal cutting blade.

Cuts for fabric strips

A straight cut with the grain is strong but ravels.

A cross cut across the grain stretches and can ravel.

A bias cut on the diagonal produces a clean but fragile edge.

Cloth strips from the same fabric cut on the length, width and bias of the fabric often look and hook differently.

When you cut cloth strips for a project, you don't need to cut them all the same width. Different widths of the same fabric can produce very different effects and enliven the piece. You can also create variety by cutting strips in a way that alters the texture of the fabric itself. For example, fabric strips cut on the length, width and bias of the material may have very different appearances—and they may also hook very differently (see pp. 49-52 for a detailed description of these variations and effects). What's important to remember is that a straight cut is the strongest, but it ravels. The cross cut often stretches more, and it can also ravel. The bias cut usually gives the most fragile strip, one that pulls apart or breaks easily. But the bias-cut strip is often the most desirable, because it doesn't ravel and it creates a clean, beautiful edge.

Some hooking needles work better with cut strips than others. Both the weight of the fabric and the width of a strip affect how easily a given strip can be hooked. Sometimes a mere $\frac{1}{32}$-in. difference in width makes a difference in the ease with which the hooking needle performs. With a little trial and error, you'll find which hooking needle works best with which weight and width of cloth strips (see pp. 35-44 for information on hooking techniques).

Although the cloth stripper can be used to cut various materials, it works best with wools, including heavy blanket-weight wools. I'm sure this tool wasn't intended for lightweight cottons, silks and satins, but I use it with them just the same. Cutting lightweight fabrics often takes patience, since the fabric may not feed well through the cutter. But once the wing nut is set with the correct pressure, the fabric cuts beautifully.

Tips for cutting
- Press all materials before cutting. Wrinkled yardage creates wrinkled strips, and yardage is much easier to press than strips.
- To test the strength and suitability of a fabric for hooking, cut a short $\frac{1}{4}$-in. strip with the scissors, and pull it between your fingers (see the photo on p. 10). If it pulls apart easily, it's usually too weak to survive the stress of a hooking needle. This is especially true with the more fragile bias cuts, loose weaves or sheer materials.
- Once you've decided a material is suitable, don't cut all the yardage at once. First test one or two short strips for strength, width and appearance. Again, $\frac{1}{32}$ in. can mean the difference between cloth strip that flows easily through the needle and one that causes trouble.
- Try to cut only what you'll use immediately. Cut strips tend to wrinkle when stored for long periods. Hanging cut strips on rods does help prevent wrinkles, but leftovers are difficult to use when you've got an odd amount.
- Use all fabric, cutting the yardage down to the last strip. Short pieces can be joined easily. When I'm desperate in mid-project because I've got only a handful of cut strips of a given fabric left, I have been known to use many strips just

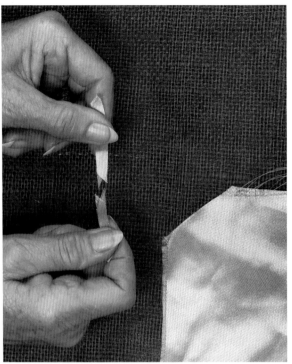

Test the strength of a fabric strip by making a short strip and pulling it between your fingers. If it pulls apart easily, as the fabric does here, it's too fragile to be used in hooking. Note that yardage tends to ravel considerably on the straight grain, somewhat on the cross grain and very little on the bias.

3 in. long, joining them with glue (see pp. 11-12 for how to do this).

- Don't cut leather or suede with the Rigby cloth stripper. Light leathers can be cut with the Strip-It, though not very efficiently, and are probably best cut with a simple razor knife. You should also avoid cutting plastics and paper with the cloth strippers. Use a paper cutter, the Olfa cutter or a pair of scissors to cut these materials.

- To protect the blades of the Rigby from dulling, always loosen the wing nut when the tool is not in use. Invariably, the handle of this tool invites passersby, particularly children, to give it a whirl. If the wing nut is not loosened, the metal blades can be dulled or damaged.

- Stagger the cutting with other work. Cutting can be a relaxing diversion from other work tasks, such as hooking or clipping, but when done over a long, uninterrupted period, it can be a tedious chore.

- If you're cutting cloth with scissors, here's a good trick that eliminates the task of joining the strips. As you're cutting the first strip of your material, stop cutting just before reaching the end (see the drawing below). Then start cutting the second strip above the first, beginning on the side opposite the side you started the first

Methods for cutting a continuous strip

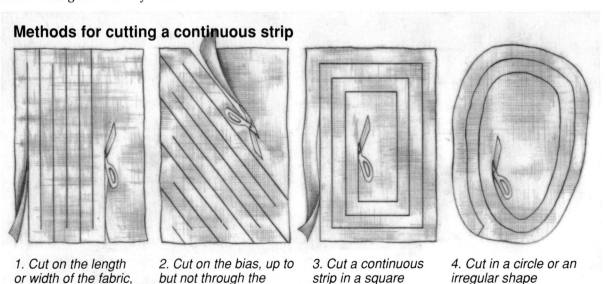

1. Cut on the length or width of the fabric, up to but not through every other side.

2. Cut on the bias, up to but not through the edge on every other row.

3. Cut a continuous strip in a square toward the center.

4. Cut in a circle or an irregular shape toward the center.

Cut strips of fabric can be joined easily by dipping one end into a small puddle of glue that you've put on a nonporous surface. When joining fabric strips, keep the overlap between strips to ⅛ in. Press the ends together tightly with your thumb and forefinger for a few seconds until the glue holds, then set aside to dry.

strip—that is, above the end you just left uncut. Again stop cutting just before reaching the end, move immediately above this uncut end and start cutting the third strip. Continue in this "zigzag" fashion, leaving just enough uncut fabric to hold the strips together. In this way you will create one long connected piece. Make sure the ends will pass through the needle. Testing one or two strips before you start cutting all the fabric is a good idea. An alternative method that produces similar results involves cutting in a spiral, as shown in the drawing.

Joining cut strips

After cutting the fabric, you'll have a stack of strips 6 in. to 6 ft. long. Imagine the awful chore of threading and rethreading your hooking needle with hundreds of short strips. The answer? Join the cut strips in a single long strand—with adhesives. The use of adhesives with fiber came as a great shock to me, but I'm sorry that this simple discovery took so many years to materialize. This method of bonding has become such an important aspect of my fiber work that I hope you, too, will take advantage of all the wondrous potential that adhesives present, not just for hooked pieces, but for all fiber construction.

Use only recommended adhesives (see the sidebar on pp. 12-14). The majority of fabric glues on the market don't work well for joining strips be-

cause they dry too slowly. Similarly, regular white glue won't work because it dries slowly and becomes too stiff. The most common brands of flexible adhesives—the desired type for joining strips—have names like Quick-Dry, Darn or Fix-So. They're always white, must dry fast and usually smell bad. They are water soluble when wet, but permanent once dry. They can be washed, and they remain flexible and hold up well.

To begin the process of joining strips, place a small drop of adhesive on a nonporous surface, such as a piece of glass, metal or plastic. As shown in the photos above, dip one corner of the strip into the glue, applying as little as possible. With the other hand, hold the strip to be joined. Spread the glue across the end in a fine white line. Overlap these two strips about ⅛ in. and squeeze the join between your thumb and forefinger tightly for three to five seconds, just long enough to get the glue to hold. This adhesive dries fast. Gently place the glued pieces to one side in small piles, allowing them to set. By the time a 12-ft. length has been glued, the bond will be strong enough to set the strip aside in a box or basket for immediate use, or to hang it on a rod or coat hanger for future use. Avoid wrinkling these strips if you want controlled, even loops. If the strips do become wrinkled, you can iron them, provided the adhesive is not exposed (in which case it would come off on the warm iron's surface plate).

Tips for gluing Joining cut strips is an easy task that can be done when you need to relax. Since it doesn't require a lot of concentration, you can do it when you're watching TV or sitting in the sun. It's also a good activity when your eyes need a break and you can't hook another inch. Here are some tips that will make your work easier and more efficient:

- Use just enough adhesive to hold. Too much glue makes the fabric too stiff to go through the needle easily. It's almost impossible to use too little glue.
- Keep the overlap to a minimum, that is, to about ⅛ in. Too much bulk from a large overlap can also make the strip stiff and prevent it from feeding freely through the needle.
- For lightweight materials like satin or cotton, use a tiny drop of glue. Heavier fabrics like wool blankets, textured materials, very absorbent fibers and some synthetics require more glue to bond. These heavier fabrics should be overlapped ¼ in. instead of the usual ⅛ in.
- After the glued strips are allowed to set up for an hour, test the bond. Gently thread them in your needle, being careful not to put any stress on the joined areas. It takes several hours for a bond to cure completely, but I'm sometimes too impatient to wait, so I test my strips to see if the bond is strong enough and then hook with care.
- Since the adhesive dries quickly, keep the bottle tightly capped when not in use.
- Consider joining strips of different colors or mixing patterns or textures for a variegated effect. By combining several similar fabrics or colors, you can extend an otherwise small amount of material to complete the job.
- Occasionally I find a fabric that won't bond easily. If it takes too much effort, I abandon it.

Adhesives

Adhesives are a modern-day wonder. They are one of my best time-saving discoveries. Not only have these compounds allowed for construction methods and techniques not possible before in fiber, but they also have eliminated endless frustration for me. Adhesives can be a great advantage for hooking enthusiasts, but they're just as useful for the weaver, knitter, sewer or anyone working in fiber.

I began to experiment with adhesives several years ago, when I received a large commission to do a work made from metal, wood, glass and plastic instead of fiber. By the time I'd found the best method of bonding these unrelated materials, I had tested over 100 types of adhesives, and I had a million new ideas. It dawned on me that I could put this technology to work for fiber.

My primary goal in terms of fiber was to find a glue to join short strips of cut yardage as well as those pieces of yarn too short to thread that I always seemed to need so desperately to finish a project. In spite of the many fiber glues on the market, very few performed well for my needs. I required a glue that would dry instantly, hold well and be invisible, permanent and washable, yet remain flexible enough to be threaded in the hooking needles. After much trial and error, I've found a selection that performs well, and the following are adhesives that I use in all my work. If your local outlet doesn't sell the specific brand, buy a small quantity of another kind and test some yourself. I consider adhesives to be my secret weapons in hooking — I hope they're just as powerful and helpful for you.

White glue
Elmer's Glue-All and Elmer's School Glue are perhaps the best-known white glues, but any brand will generally work. When dry, white glue is firm and stiff but washable, and holds up well. This adhesive secures knots and bonds many materials to a hooked surface — synthetics that

Adhesives for rug hooking include (left to right) Elmer's white glue, often used diluted to seal edges and mend holes; flexible adhesives, used to join cut fabric strips (first group of four) and those with a stronger bond used to secure hems and attach unusual materials (next group of four); household cement (next group of two); and latex, another flexible glue, used to seal the backing of a finished piece.

are difficult to work with, suede, leather, wood, screws and paper. However, white glue is not satisfactory for joining cut fabric strips because it doesn't dry fast enough. Water soluble when wet, it dries permanent and clear overnight. Don't cover large areas of your work with white glue, since it often cracks the fiber.

White glue is thinned by mixing about one part white glue to ten parts water. This diluted solution is applied to cut edges as sizing to prevent raveling, to hems to make them firm before stitching them and to weak areas for reinforcement during mending. Use this diluted solution when you want a degree of stiffness tempered with some flexibility. Thinned white glue mixes well with water-based paints for areas needing color or filling. The consistency is easily changed to fit the needs of a given situation by adding more or less water. The diluted solution dries permanent and clear (unless mixed with paints) in 6 to 12 hours.

Household cement
Duco and Bond 527 are some of the many brands of household cement available on the market. All are clear, fast-drying and strong. They're nonsoluble, brittle when dry, permanent and

washable. A thin coat can set up in 15 minutes and be fully cured in 24 hours. Household cement is the best adhesive I've found to anchor nonfiber materials like wire, monofilament, metallic yarns or cords and metal elements to hooked works.

Flexible adhesives
Flexible adhesives, as their name suggests, allow fiber and fabric to remain pliable once the adhesive has dried, an advantage when hooking with joined cut strips. I prefer water-soluble flexible adhesives that dry clear and permanent.

Quick-Dry Adhesive, Darn, Fix-So, Stitchless Fabric Glue and Fabric Mender Magic are fast-drying adhesives that work best for joining cut yardage strips and yarn. These adhesives stay pliable, yet are permanent when dry and washable. Water-soluble when wet, they dry clear in about 30 seconds. Purchase one tube at a time, since they have a short shelf life.

Tacky Glue is an adhesive that's great for hems, especially those with mitered corners. This glue cures in 6 to 24 hours, allows good control and bonds well. It's thick and easy to spread, and it's water-soluble when wet. It dries clear and permanent and is washable. I like to use this adhesive for an instant bond when I want a flexible glue. It works well for securing cut cloth shag to the backing material (see p. 64).

Super Tacky has the same properties as Tacky Glue but is thicker. It's good for applying large, heavy objects like plastics and metal elements. It dries clear and permanent in four to eight hours.

Touch Down Kwik Seam and Jasco Stop-Slip are brands of latex adhesive, and there are many others available from any carpet-supply outlet. Latex is applied to rug backing to hold loops secure as well as make the rugs skid-proof. It's always applied full-strength. The thick, rubberized adhesive is water-soluble when wet but dries permanent, clear and waterproof overnight. Latex dissolves in dry-cleaning solutions and may have to be reapplied if rugs are sent out for professional dry cleaning.

Choosing and using adhesives

How do you choose which adhesive to use? If you understand the properties of each, you'll find it easier to determine which glue is appropriate. Consider factors such as control, stiffness or flexibility, drying time and ease of application. Keep in mind that new adhesives with better bonding properties come on the market every year. The best approach is to test on small areas to be sure the adhesive will work for your needs.

As a general rule, don't use household cements and undiluted white glue on a large area of fiber since they don't allow the fabric to remain soft and flexible. Use the flexible adhesives instead (Tacky, Quick-Dry or Latex).

Most water-soluble adhesives are best applied with a soft brush. Latex, which is thicker, needs a small spatula or plastic knife to spread it over the backing. Brushes should be washed well in warm, soapy water after use so they won't stiffen up permanently and become unusable. A glue gun is another option, but I find it too hard to control. A glue gun does allow adhesive to adhere quickly and set up fast, however—a decided advantage.

Backing materials

The backing (the material on which the hooking is worked) serves as the foundation for the finished piece. For this reason, the choice of fabric for backing is important. It must be strong enough to withstand the process of hooking, during which it will be punched, poked and stretched repeatedly.

Almost any strong, open-weave fabric that will accept the hooking needles easily can be used, including linen, cotton, monk's cloth, cotton/polyester blends, synthetics and burlap. Look for a fabric woven with a density of 10 epi (ends per inch). To determine epi, lay the cloth flat, place a ruler on it and count the threads in an inch (see the drawing below). A fabric with 10 to 12 epi with a strong, open weave hooks best, since it accepts loops most readily. (In regular hooking, loops are placed in every hole in the backing.) Backing with threads closer together makes it difficult to push the needle through; a looser weave spaces loops out too far, making it difficult to achieve a firm hooked surface. Backing need not be prewashed.

Plastic-coated canvas, plastic-coated scrim and needlepoint canvas are not recommended for rug hooking. These materials either have an incorrect weave for hooking or they don't "give" when the needle enters the surface.

Fiber density, or ends per inch

Sample weave worked at 10 threads per inch (10 epi)   2 4 6 8 10

Fiber density is measured in ends per inch (epi). This number indicates the quantity of threads in 1 in. of fabric. The larger the number, the tighter the weave. For rug-hooking purposes, an epi of 10 is desirable.

With regard to color, I prefer a natural or white backing material, which will not interfere visually with the colors of yarn and fabrics being hooked. I try to select a fabric suited for the particular demands of the project. To determine these needs, I ask myself how the work will be used. If as a rug, will it be used on the floor or will it be treated like a wall hanging? Is the piece wearable? Is it to be washable? Answers to such questions guide me in selecting a backing material. More often than not, these materials have to be ordered by mail, but I constantly keep my eyes open for any possibilities in fabric and upholstery stores. In order of preference, the following are fabrics I most frequently use for backing materials:

Linen

Linen is definitely my favorite backing material. It's strong, pleasing to the touch and wonderful to work with. But it's also expensive and difficult to find. The lighter weights of linen are suitable for most projects, such as wall hangings, pillows or wearables. If you can afford it, use a heavier weight and better quality for floor rugs. But keep in mind the relationship of cost between the backing and hooking materials. It seems a bit ridiculous to make an entire rug from scraps or remnants that are free, only to spend $50 to $75 for backing material. With the trend toward more natural fibers, linen has become more readily available at better prices and is now a good choice for a backing material.

Linen is washable, comes in widths up to 60 in. and is available in natural and white. I purchase it by mail order, where I can obtain high quality for better prices than I generally find in stores.

Cotton

My current favorite backing for floor rugs is a very heavy, sturdy, 100% cotton that resembles woven string. Although cotton is softer than other fabrics, this weave is strong enough to keep stretching to a minimum. Cotton backing is washable and comes in a natural color. Better grades for hooking are available by mail order in widths from 60 in. to 120 in. For most large projects, the 120-in. width offers the tremendous advantage of eliminating the tedious task of seaming or piecing narrow widths of backing.

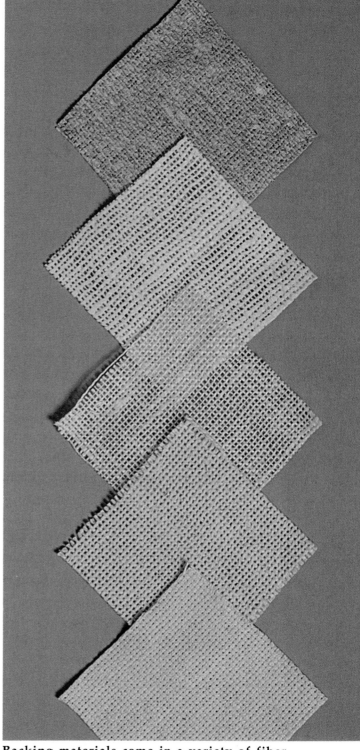

Backing materials come in a variety of fiber contents and weaves, including (top to bottom) natural-colored linen, medium-weight white linen, lightweight white linen, heavy cotton and cotton monk's cloth.

Additional backing materials are (top to bottom) open-weave cotton, cotton/polyester blend, open-weave synthetic and burlap, in two of its many bright colors.

Monk's cloth

This material—named for its common use in monk's habits—is a two-ply, medium-weight, 100% cotton in a basketweave. It was among the first commercial weaves for rug hooking and has been in use now for more than 50 years. It's readily available and is the most common choice of backings for rug-hooking enthusiasts. It's suitable for most hooked projects but tends to stretch while being worked, which makes tightening a necessity from time to time (see pp. 28-31 for information on stretching the canvas). Recently, it's become difficult to find monk's cloth in anything other than a wide 5-epi weave, which is not as satisfactory as the traditional firmer weave.

This backing is washable and comes in a natural color and a range of widths—55 in., 92 in., 184 in. and 220 in. It can be purchased by mail order.

Cotton/polyester monk's cloth

A fairly new "monk's cloth" made of a two-ply blend of cotton and polyester can usually be found in major fabric chains at a very reasonable price. Because it's quite stiff, however, it takes a bit of getting used to to keep the needles in the holes, hook with the grain and follow straight lines. I like the fact that it does not stretch as much as the 100%-cotton version. Several types of fabric are referred to as monk's cloth, so make sure to find one that measures 10 to 12 epi and has an even basketweave. Cotton/polyester monk's cloth is washable, comes in a natural color in 55-in. widths and is available at most fabric stores.

Synthetics

Synthetics work well as backing material, but they're hard to find with the necessary density of 10 to 12 epi and a sturdy, plain, open weave. Upholstery and drapery shops often carry synthetic materials that are worth investigating. Synthetics appropriate for backing material are usually washable. They're usually available in white or a natural color and come in widths of 55 in. to 60 in.

Burlap

Burlap, a fiber made from jute, was one of the earliest materials used for hooked rugs. Traditional rug hookers used grain sacks of burlap to fashion their works, and the even, open weave of burlap made it popular among those early hooking enthusiasts. Today, burlap is inexpensive and readily available. Unfortunately, it is very fragile and has a rough texture, which makes it undesirable to use. It breaks easily and weakens from the effects of sun, heat or moisture. It's not recommended by textile experts for any long-lasting work. Nevertheless, I use burlap for certain projects—mainly for wearables where I want a color that's unavailable in other backings. I frankly don't care if some of my work won't be around by the year 3000, just as I'm sure it won't end up in the Metropolitan Museum's vault.

The main reason I do occasionally use burlap is to take advantage of the wonderful color range it offers. My work depends on creating many visual dimensions or levels. By exposing the unhooked ground cloth, I gain one more level, one more texture, in a satisfying color. Burlap is also good value in terms of cost, and it's readily available at any yard-goods store.

Now that latex is available, it may be questionable whether burlap is all that fragile. This backing compound (see pp. 112-113) not only locks the fibers of the hooked materials to the ground cloth but also prevents exposure of the finished work to the damaging effects of light, moisture and soil. But before I talk anyone into my least favorite backing material, I must admit that the only time I use it is in small personal items, like a vest or a pair of slippers. I never use it for public works, rugs or wall hangings, because it doesn't have the value or quality I want for such pieces.

When shopping for burlap, it's important to be selective, since it comes in many qualities. Once you've bought burlap yardage, be sure to look it over carefully when you're getting ready to cut it for stretching on the frame. Avoid areas with broken threads, thin spots and uneven slub weaves. Because this fiber can be irritating to the skin, it's wise to cover your bare arms when working on any large or lengthy project.

Most burlap is not washable, although there are a growing number of burlaps on the market that can be washed carefully by hand. (They lose a bit of the sizing during washing.) Washable burlap and nonwashable burlap come in many colors and in widths of 50 in. to 60 in. Burlap can be purchased by mail order or in fabric stores.

Frames

In order to hook the backing material, it must be attached to a frame that provides a strong supporting structure for the work in progress. Frames vary in size from small lap frames—so named because you work seated, with the frame resting in your lap—to larger standing and upright frames. Frames can be purchased or made by hand. In the latter case, they can be made from raw lumber or from an existing frame like a window frame, or they can be constructed from stretcher strips used for painting canvases.

Whether you purchase a commercial frame or fabricate your own, your rug-hooking frame should be sturdy enough to withstand the tension placed on it by the taut backing material and the repeated pressure during hooking. It should also be a comfortable size to work with—large enough to provide ample room to hook, but not so large that it becomes cumbersome. Ideally, the frame should be large enough for you to complete the entire hooked piece without having to make it in sections. (Hooking pieces larger than the overall frame means that they must be done one section at a time, removed from the frame, rolled up, then moved to complete the next section. See p. 23 for more information on this.) In general, frames larger than 3 ft. should be standing or upright frames, since they become too heavy to use efficiently as lap frames.

Lap frames

Lap frames are available commercially, or they can easily be constructed from precut wood strips sold as painting stretcher frames. These wooden strips resemble picture frames and are sold by the pair at art-supply stores in lengths up to 40 in. (lengths up to 60 in. can usually be special-ordered). Two pairs (four strips total) are needed for each frame, and the pairs can be the same or different lengths, depending on your choice of a square or rectangular frame. The four sides are easily assembled by pushing the notched corners together. Because no nails or hardware are required, they are easily assembled, and can be disassembled for storage.

A big advantage of these lightweight frames is their portability. By resting the top of the frame on

Small frames can be constructed from precut wooden stretcher strips used to make painting canvases. The strips are sold in pairs of various lengths and are prenotched for easy assembly, as shown at top. To assemble frames from stretcher strips, just push the notched edges together so they interlock securely and their mitered edges meet (above). Since no nails or other fasteners are used, the strips can later be disassembled for reuse.

the edge of a table and the lower end on your lap, a comfortable working position is possible. These frames can be turned around in any direction for easier hooking and also turned over so that you can view the right side of your work. (As you'll see in Chapter 2, most hooking is worked on the wrong side of the backing material.) These stretcher frames are also great for traveling. In fact, I often measure my suitcase, then select a frame to fit it. Stretcher frames are also ideal for students and for workshops.

A good size for beginning projects is 21 in. by 24 in., which means that you need to buy a pair of stretcher strips 21 in. long and a pair 24 in. long. The wood frame itself is 2 in. wide, leaving a maximum hooking area (the open space inside the frame) of about 17 in. by 20 in. Since you can't hook right up to the edge of the frame because the needle would hit the wood, the real workable area probably measures 15 in. by 18 in. This is a good size for a sofa pillow or a small wall hanging.

In addition to its size restrictions, the other disadvantage of this type of frame is that it necessitates the use of thumbtacks to hold and stretch the backing material. Even though tacking does not take that long, I find this part of any hooking project the most distasteful. Since you need to keep your backing material taut during the entire hooking process, taking these tacks out to restretch the backing is an added annoyance. I know of several people who use staples to secure the backing material, but I don't like the damage they do to the wood frames. One alternative to thumbtacks or staples is tack stripping (see pp. 21-22).

Standing, or upright, frames

Projects that require frames larger than 3 ft. should be hooked on standing, or upright, frames. These can be purchased as commercial frames, fabricated from structures like old windows or doors, or constructed from raw lumber.

Several commercial frames are available, including tilting floor frames and horizontal frames. These frames are usually small (sized only up to about 40 in. in length or width) and are often expensive. Also, when filled with a densely hooked project, commercial frames can become top-heavy and unsteady. I much prefer making frames from lumber, from picture or window frames or from

This commercial tilting frame, which works best for lightweight pieces, expands to a maximum of 30 in. by 40 in. by moving its wooden braces in the predrilled holes.

precut stretcher strips, which are readily available at art-supply stores.

Picture frames were the frames I used when I first started hooking. I happily made several projects on them until I finally outgrew their small size. Any sturdy wooden frame in which you don't mind placing thumbtacks or nails can work well as a rug-hooking frame. An early favorite of mine that I still use is an antique window frame. The leaded glass has been removed, leaving a far stronger frame than many that are available today. A wooden screen door with the screen removed would work as well.

After trying every type of frame, I have decided that I like making frames from raw lumber best (for details on how to build them, see pp. 21-23). Raw lumber offers the greatest flexibility in terms of size and is generally the least expensive frame to make. With planning, the frames can be de-

A sturdy wooden door or window frame can be used for hooking large pieces. Be sure to remove all glass and debris from the frame, as the author is doing here with a chisel.

Basic materials needed to make rug-hooking frames include (top to bottom) knot-free wood stock in either 2-in. by 2-in. or 2-in. by 3-in. widths, tack stripping, corner braces and corner-brace screws. Tools include a hammer, tape measure and screwdriver, as well as work gloves to protect the hands from tack stripping.

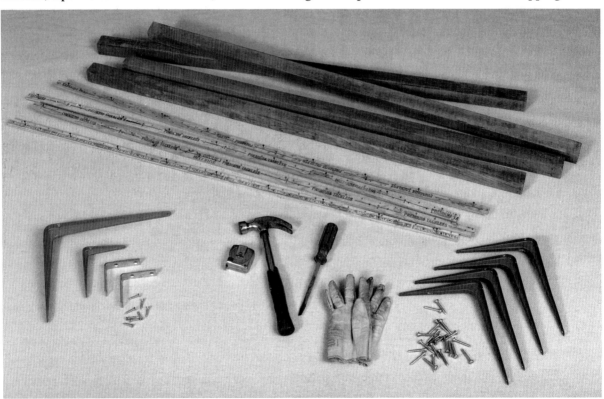

signed for reuse in future projects of different sizes. And the larger sizes can be used by two or more people hooking at the same time.

Besides eliminating the chore of repositioning sections of a seamed canvas on the frame, the main advantage of a large frame is that it enables you to see the entire design as you work. It's much easier to work with the total image in view rather than having to guess what's happening in the rolled-up section that you completed months before. I laugh now when I think of the 9-ft. wide rug I made years ago on a 30-in. by 40-in. tilting floor frame. Can you begin to imagine the problems? The weight of the almost-completed rug became so great that I had to secure the rolled-up sections with rope tied to the ceiling. Even worse, I had to try and remember what the work inside that huge roll looked like, since it had been completed months before. I ended up ripping out half the long weeks of work, replacing colors and improving the bad design. It was the last time I used that approach.

Of course, if your project is really large, it may not be practical to make a frame large enough without rolling under a section. I make my frames the maximum size that I can still lift, turn and manage myself. To date, this is a 7-ft. by 8-ft. frame made of 2-in. by 3-in. wood. In spite of the added weight of a finished rug on the frame, I can still move this size to any position necessary. And it's surprising how often all these frames need to be moved and turned.

Constructing a frame

Just as for making frames from precut stretcher strips, you can easily construct frames from four lengths of 2-in. by 2-in. or 2-in. by 3-in. wood stock, either all the same size or two pairs cut to different lengths. Any length can be used, bearing in mind the limitations on frame size discussed above. In addition to the lumber, you'll need four shelf supports to join the corners and heavy-duty screws 1½ in. long for attaching them to the frame.

I don't recommend using 4x4 lumber for frames; it's simply too heavy. Most of my frames are made from surplus wood, like pieces left over from building our house. If you need to purchase new lumber, look for clear stock with few or no knots (knots weaken the wood). If the lumberyard car-

ries only long lengths, they'll cut pieces to the desired lengths for a small fee. No sanding or sealing is needed for wood used as frames.

As you progress in your rug-hooking work, you'll quickly learn that a tightly stretched backing material is mandatory and that tightening and straightening the fabric is necessary from time to time. Using tack stripping instead of the traditional thumbtacks or staples makes restretching the fabric much easier. Tack stripping, also called Tackless Carpet Stripping, is a 1-in. wide wood strip with very sharp tacks protruding at an angle through the surface at ¾-in. intervals. Available in 4-ft. lengths at any carpet-installation firm, tack stripping is nailed to the back surface of the frame to hold the backing material on the frame. When the tack stripping is in place, restretching the canvas is done by simply lifting the material off the tack points, pulling it tight and straight, and placing it back on the tack-strip points.

When constructing frames, you will need enough tack stripping to cover each length of wood. The tack strip is nailed to the 2-in. by 2-in.

Large frames are constructed by screwing corner braces to individual lengths of wood. The frame is then assembled by joining the other half of the corner brace to the adjacent length of wood.

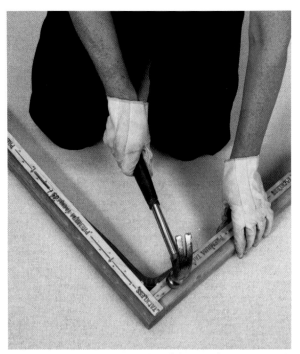

wood frame, with the tacks slanting outward, away from the frame. It's the slant of the tacks that holds the backing material on the frame. Saw any excess lengths of tack stripping off to save for other frames.

A word of caution: Whenever you use tack stripping, be sure to protect yourself by placing some covering over those vicious, sharp tacks. A folded cloth or a piece of narrow cardboard or sponge rubber can be pinned around the edge. The best method I've found is to cover the tack stripping with a 1-in. to 2-in. strip of ½-in. thick Foam Core, a spongelike material sandwiched between layers of white plasticized cardboard. Available in art-supply stores, Foam Core stays in place and covers the points perfectly.

Determining the size of frame and materials

When you are determining frame size, remember that the inside measurement (work area) requires 1 in. to 2 in. extra allowance on all sides, since it's not possible to hook up to the very edge of the frame. For example, a finished piece measuring 16 in. by 20 in. should be hooked on a frame no

Hammered to the back of large frames, tack stripping, with its sharp protruding points, provides an easy means of attaching backing material to the frame.

Determining frame size and amount of backing needed

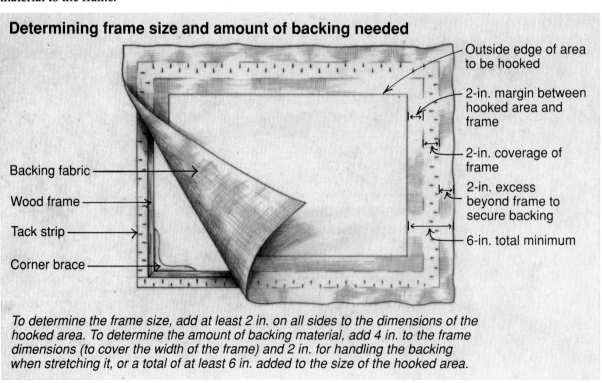

- Outside edge of area to be hooked
- 2-in. margin between hooked area and frame
- 2-in. coverage of frame
- 2-in. excess beyond frame to secure backing
- 6-in. total minimum

Backing fabric

Wood frame

Tack strip

Corner brace

To determine the frame size, add at least 2 in. on all sides to the dimensions of the hooked area. To determine the amount of backing material, add 4 in. to the frame dimensions (to cover the width of the frame) and 2 in. for handling the backing when stretching it, or a total of at least 6 in. added to the size of the hooked area.

smaller than 20 in. by 24 in. Also, the larger the frame, the larger the corner braces must be. Generally, a 6-ft. by 8-ft. frame needs corner braces measuring 10 in. by 12 in. or 12 in. by 14 in.

You may find that larger frames start to bend or bow in from so much stretch and stress. This tendency is easily corrected by adding a movable center support. Cut a length of wood the same length as the inside measurement of the frame it needs to brace. Since this piece is not permanent, it can be moved if it prevents viewing or access to the active work area.

I get very impatient when I have many screws to set, so I leave a set of L-shaped shelf supports permanently screwed onto the edge of each length of wood. In this way I have to screw on only one half of the bracket when attaching the other length of lumber to change frame sizes. These shelf supports are so inexpensive that using them is a pleasurable luxury. Also, I always use the same size screws so that the holes for the screws can be predrilled, making installation easy.

After you've determined the frame size, you must calculate the amount of backing material needed. The backing fabric must be large enough to complete the project and be well secured to the frame. A minimum margin of 6 in. around the hooked work is required. This 6-in. margin allows for the wood-frame interference (generally 2 in.), since you can't hook to the very edge; 2 in. to cover the wood frame; and 2 in. used to stretch and secure the backing to the frame. For example, a finished work measuring 16 in. by 20 in. that is to be hooked on a 20-in. by 24-in. frame will need a piece of backing material at least 22 in. by 26 in. The drawing on the facing page provides a diagram of the calculations and amount of material that is required.

Preparing backing material for stretching

Once you've calculated how much backing material is needed, it's time to prepare the material for stretching on the frame. In most cases, you'll purchase an ample length of fabric to complete a given project or enough to do several projects. If you can avoid it, don't cut the material to fit the frame, particularly for large frames where tack stripping is used. The excess material can be tightly rolled, then pinned over the tack stripping, serving as a convenient protective cover as well as eliminating any waste of the precious backing material, which can be used for future projects. With large frames, it's not uncommon to roll up one to two yards of excess fabric tightly without causing any problems. The extra cloth also gives better leverage for holding when stretching the fabric on the frame. However, rolling up the excess fabric is inadvisable with small lap frames, where the bulk of a large roll of fabric would make hooking difficult.

Seaming, or piecing
Ideally, you should always have enough backing material so that seams are unnecessary, but this isn't always possible. For example, 50-in. wide material is insufficient for making a 65-in. sq. hanging, so two or more pieces of backing must be sewn together.

Seaming, or piecing, backing material is done for one of two reasons, the more common reason being to provide sufficient backing for the area being hooked. The other reason for piecing is if your backing is large enough for the hooked area but too small to cover the frame when stretched. In this case, you need to seam two, or even four, small backing extensions to the larger canvas.

Whatever the reason for piecing, remember that the backing material — and any seams — will be subject to great stress when the piece is stretched on the frame. Seams must therefore be worked on a sewing machine — never by hand — and be strong enough not to pull out or separate. It's a good idea to double-stitch the seams; with open weaves, it's crucial to reinforce the seams with two or three rows of stitching.

Seaming selvages requires clipping the backing fabric every 5 in. to 6 in. to release the tightly woven edge and prevent the finished seam from puckering (above). Then, with pieces pinned every 3 in. to 4 in., the backing fabric is stretched to its maximum as it is fed through the sewing machine to prevent puckering (below).

When sewing two sections together on the machine, stretch them both to their maximum to prevent the stitching from drawing in when the backing is stretched on the frame. As you seam, firmly pull the unstitched material in front of the needle toward you with one hand and at the same time, pull the seamed material behind the needle away from you.

When piecing backing sections, it's easiest to seam at the selvages, since the edges line up and will not ravel. However, take care to keep the stretch on these seams the same as that in the body of the fabric. Selvages are always woven more tightly than the main fabric and hence do not stretch as much as the rest of the fabric. To equalize the stretch, clip the selvage edge every 5 in. to 6 in., but only within the seam allowance, not into the line of stitching.

This will release the tightly woven edge. Pin the selvages every 3 in. to 4 in., matching the grain as perfectly as possible. Stretch the selvages to their maximum with both hands (as described above), using a straight (not zigzag) stitch on the sewing machine. Try to align the stitching as exactly as possible with the grain thread. Reinforce this seam with one or two more rows of stitching, using the same maximum stretch. You'll quickly see the importance of stretching once the fabric is mounted on the frame, because a tight seam will prove difficult to pull even with the rest of the surface.

The seaming requirements vary slightly, depending on whether you're piecing the backing within the hooking area or simply adding temporary extensions to cover the frame. If you're piecing within the hooking area, it's important to join only the same types of backing fabrics. In other words, don't add a piece of linen to a piece of burlap. The weave and stretch of each fabric is different, and, surprisingly enough, these differences show dramatically when unmatched backings are hooked. Also try to match the lengths or widths of the pieces of fabric you're joining, since the stretch may be greater in one direction than the other. This is less important for even, plain weaves whose stretch is fairly uniform, but it's still a good idea to get in the habit of matching not only the fabric but also the direction of the weave.

All seams should be made on the working side of the canvas, so that they will be invisible on the right side of the piece. Sew plain seams—never flat-fell or overlapping seams—with a straight stitch and a minimum of ⅝-in. allowance. Nothing is more heartbreaking than having the ridge of a seam line show in a finished piece, and no amount of steam pressing will flatten an overlapped or flat-fell seam or straighten a plain seam that has been sewn haphazardly.

Before seaming, consider the design to determine where the seam can be most easily concealed. Each design must be handled individually, but the general idea is to try to integrate the seam lines into the design so that the seams coincide with either a horizontal or vertical pattern. The easiest seam to camouflage is one under a high-shag or high-looped surface, and less care need be taken when seaming if the seamed area is to be hooked exclusively with this technique. The most difficult seam to hide is a very flat, hooked pile. Keeping the seam in line with the design for such hooked areas is the best way to conceal it.

If you are seaming temporary extensions to the backing material to enlarge it enough to cover the frame, the most important thing to remember is that seaming should always be done before mounting the backing to the frame. Occasionally when I've gotten a terrific idea in mid-project that involves enlarging a corner or an edge, I've added extensions after finishing the main hooking, but this is very difficult to do, and I don't advise it.

Since these extensions are temporary, you need not match the backing fabric exactly, as you must for piecing within the hooking area. It's nonetheless a good idea for all the pieces to have the same amount of stretch, so the tension will be the same overall when the backing and extensions are stretched on the frame. For this reason, I save scraps of backing fabric from each project that I complete and use them over and over again for extensions. These extensions should be sewn onto the backing with at least a ⅝-in. overlapping seam, using either two or three rows of zigzag or straight stitching.

Seaming with diagonal, or bias, designs

As you can see from much of my work, I love diagonal lines. Because I find it much easier to hook with the grain on the straight of the material rather than to hook on the diagonal, I always

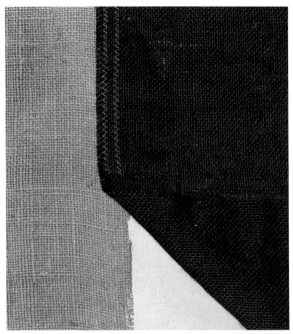

stretch the backing for these bias designs diagonally on the frame. That way I can hook on the straight grain but retain my diagonal design.

Sometimes my large works with diagonal designs, like *Metro-Plex* (see p. 89), need to have a pieced backing. In such cases, I seam the backing sections on the straight grain or with the selvages together — just as I would for piecing any backing for the hooking area — and then turn the entire pieced backing diagonally on the frame. When stretching the backing on the frame, I make sure the seams of the pieced sections line up with the diagonal lines of the design in my cartoon. (Because the stretch of the straight grain and bias are so different, I never combine pieced backing sections positioned on the straight grain with others positioned on the bias since the hooked work would never lie flat.)

When you are working with designs that have large diagonal elements, you'll find this design approach speeds up your work. Hooking on the bias is very slow and tedious when precision is important, whereas hooking on the straight grain is fast and wonderful.

If your backing material is not large enough, you can stitch extensions to the main piece with overlapping seams by using a few rows of zigzag stitching. The fabric need not be the same color but should have the same weight and amount of stretch.

Piecing a several-part diagonal design

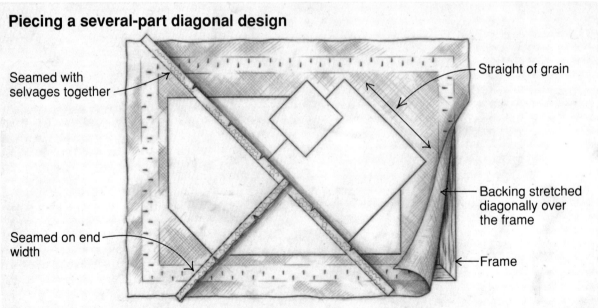

Seamed with selvages together

Straight of grain

Seamed on end width

Backing stretched diagonally over the frame

Frame

This sketch of Metro-Plex *stretched diagonally on the frame shows how the author seams her large bias designs on the straight grain to facilitate hooking. She conceals the seams by placing them on design lines (the finished piece is shown on p. 89).*

Diluted white glue is used to seal the threads of the backing material (above) to prevent raveling once the fabric is cut. Once the glue has dried, the cut material (right) leaves a crisp, clean edge that doesn't ravel.

Protecting edges from raveling

Nothing is more frustrating than fighting raveling threads, as you watch your backing slip away while your hooking progresses. Because backing fabrics are an open weave, they have a strong tendency to ravel. I use several means to prevent this, most of them worked before the fabric is placed on the frame.

My favorite method involves adhesive (see the sidebar on pp. 12-14 for detailed information on adhesives). I use a diluted wash of white glue on the raw edges of the backing. This works best if the fabric is stretched flat and the glue is applied and allowed to dry completely before using. This is also a good technique to use before cutting any piece of the backing material in two. Protect the fabric and the tabletop with a clean piece of plastic. Don't use anything with colored printing on it, for it may bleed onto your material. Use a 2-in. brush to spread diluted adhesive across the area to be cut. Let the glue dry completely (usually overnight), then cut in the center of the glued area, evenly and on grain. Both edges—one for use now and one for a later work—are now sealed, leaving a slightly stiff edge that's free from ravels.

With heavier fabrics, other methods may work better. A rule of thumb is that the heavier the fabric, the thicker the glue needs to be. A bit of exper-

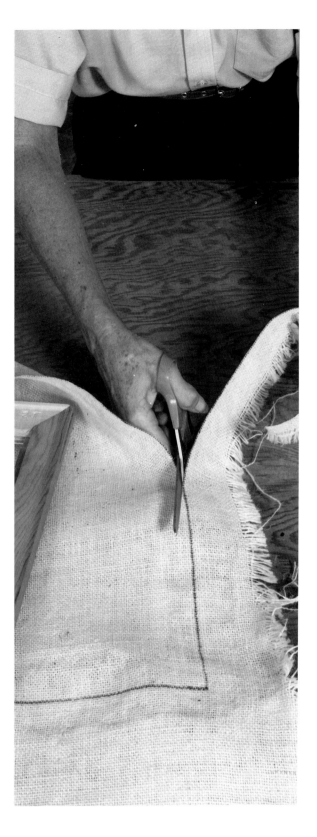

Two other options for preventing raveling include zigzag-stitching the edges (left edge of fabric) or wrapping the edges with masking tape (right edge).

Stretching the backing on the frame

Seeing a limp pile of fabric before it's attached to the frame can be terribly intimidating, but once that first edge is secured, the frustration passes. Remember that you'll be hooking on the back of

1 The process of stretching the backing begins by laying the backing material flat and positioning the frame on top, allowing enough room at the edges to fold the material over the frame. Be sure to line up the straight of the fabric grain with one side of the frame (the grain line here is stitched in dark yarn for clarity's sake). First, tack the fabric at one corner of the frame. Then, keeping the grain line parallel to the frame, tack the fabric at the center and other corner of the frame. (If thumbtacks can't be pushed in easily, use a hammer to tap them in.) Then add tacks between these three at 2-in. intervals.

the design and fabric, so the back of any seams in the backing material should be facing you.

To ensure successful and enjoyable hooking, the backing must be stretched onto the frame as tight and as straight as possible. Controlling the loops in hooking is very difficult on a slack foundation, and it's a constant challenge to keep the backing as taut as possible. In fact, the backing can never be stretched too tight.

Backing is stretched on all frames in basically the same manner. The backing material is secured at one corner, then stretched along one edge, aligned with the grain. Then, the opposite side of the material is stretched and secured. The third and final sides of the canvas are then stretched (see the photos on the facing page and below).

The main difference between approaches to stretching is in the method of securing the backing

2 Pulling the fabric as taut as possible, stretch the backing over the opposite edge of the frame, fold it back over the edge and place a tack at the center of this side. Then, moving 2 in. to the right of the center tack, again pull the fabric as taut as possible, keeping the grain and frame aligned, and add a second tack. Move to the left of the center tack and repeat this process. Working back and forth in this way across the entire edge of the frame, place tacks about 2 in. apart, finishing with a tack in each corner.

3 Continue around the third and fourth sides, tacking about every 2 in. across each edge, pulling the fabric taut and making sure the grain lines stay straight.

4 Fold the extra edges under at corners and secure with a thumbtack.

5 The back of this frame shows the neat edges and proper alignment of the fabric grain on the frame. Since hooking will be done from the other side, the fabric seen here on the interior of the frame becomes the front of the finished work.

Stretching the backing on large frames is generally done on a large table or on the floor, in just the same way as for small frames. Here the author has completed stretching the first side and secures the opposite corner, bracing the frame with her foot to achieve a tight stretch on the backing fabric.

to the frame. You can use either thumbtacks or tack stripping. I suggest using thumbtacks only for the smaller frames but prefer the ease and speed of tack stripping, especially for stretching backing on larger frames.

If you do use thumbtacks, a small screwdriver is good for removing them and saves fingers and fingernails. As I mentioned before, some students prefer to use staples for small frames, but the disadvantage is that they mar the frames.

Expect to restretch your backing, since it's difficult to get the grain lined up perfectly with the initial tacking, and the backing stretches during the hooking process. Once the fabric is even and tight, roll up any excess material tightly and secure it with pins over the tack stripping for protection. Any edge with tacks exposed must be covered. Use a strip of cardboard, the roll of fabric, Styrofoam or Foam Core (my favorite) to cover any exposed tacks. With your backing material stretched tightly on the frame, excess fabric secured and any exposed tacks covered, you're ready to begin to hook.

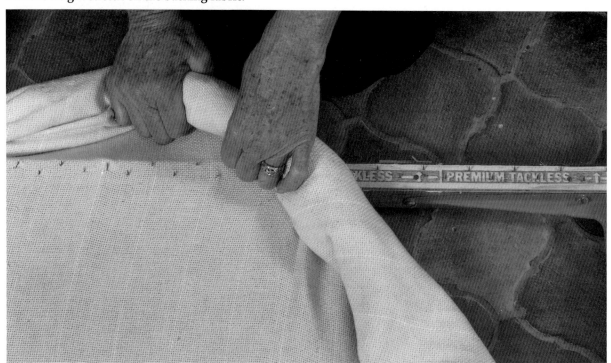

Tack stripping allows easy adjustment of backing fabric when it becomes too loose or when a large piece needs to be repositioned on the frame. The protruding tacks slant outward, holding the fabric in place.

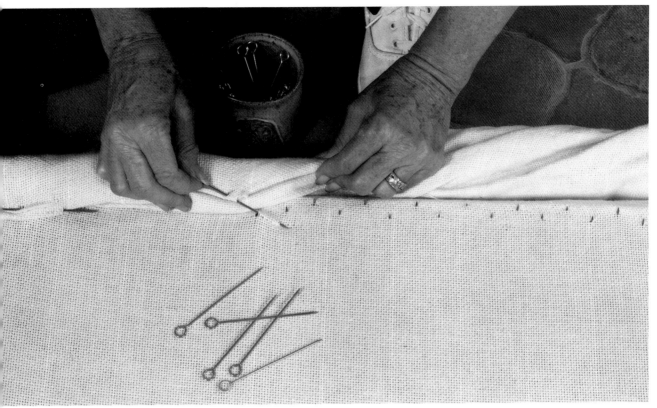

After stretching the backing, roll up the excess fabric and pin it in place to provide a protective covering over the tack stripping.

Narrow strips of ¼-in. thick Foam Core protect fingers from the protruding points of tack stripping. The Foam Core is anchored to the frame with large thumbtacks.

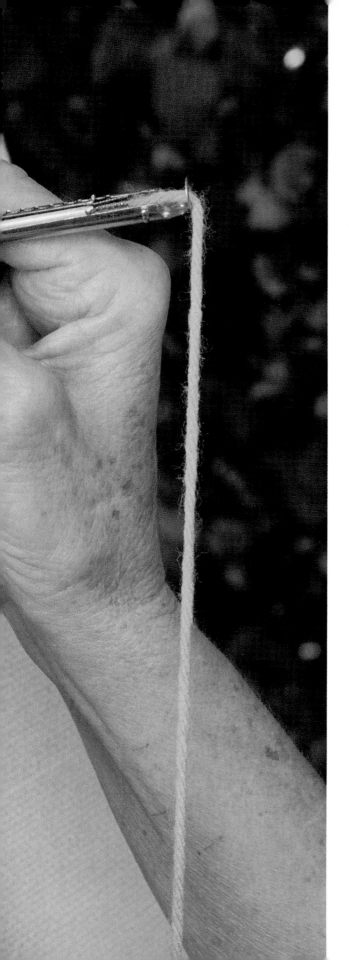

Basic Tools and Techniques

One of the marvelous things about rug hooking is the simplicity of the tools and techniques involved. In the 30 years that I have been working in this craft, two rug-hooking needles—the punch needle and the speed needle—have served as the basis for my work. Many variations can be obtained using just these two inexpensive tools (which are shown in the photos on p. 34). You will quickly see how experimentation will lead to mixing techniques, materials and textures.

The punch needle consists of a handle and two interchangeable needles. The large needle is used for heavy rug yarns or for cut wool or cotton yardage strips, while the small needle is used for lighter-weight yarns like four-ply knitting worsted, sport yarns or cords. The handle of the

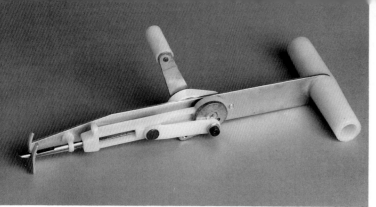
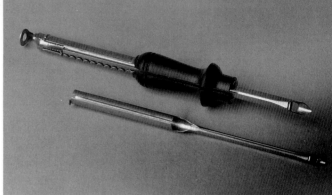

The speed needle (at left) and the punch needle (at right) both simply make loops in a backing canvas, but they offer endless possibilities because they can vary the loop length and be used with many materials.

punch needle is equipped with ten notches and a slide lock that moves up and down in the handle to hold the needle in the desired place. Locking the needle into different notches varies the length of the loops from ⅛ in. to ¾ in.

I have a punch needle that's 30 years old, dating to the time I was first introduced to rug hooking, and this tool is still one of my favorites. Indeed, the punch needle is preferred by many rug hookers because adjustments can be made on it so easily. It's also popular because it's easy to manage, quiet, relaxing to use, inexpensive and versatile.

The speed needle, sometimes called the hand needle, is the other most common rug-hooking needle. It operates like an eggbeater, automatically moving forward and forming loops as the handle is turned in a clockwise motion. The loops can be easily adjusted to five different lengths by moving the setscrew into any of five different holes opposite the handle. Loops can range in size from ⅛ in. to ¾ in. long — the same range as with the punch needle. The fact that the speed needle has only five increments in size rather than ten is a minor limitation that has never bothered me at all.

The punch needle and its assembly

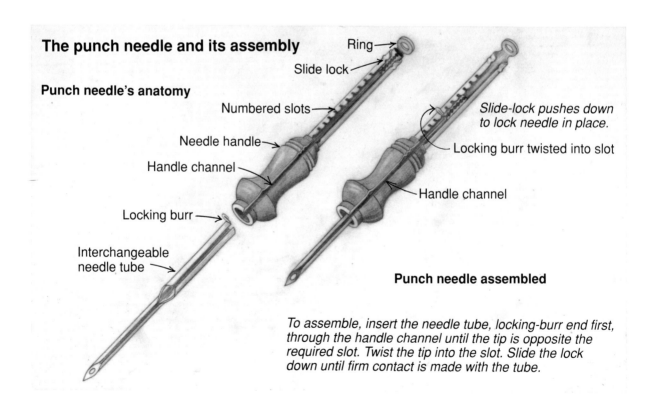

Punch needle's anatomy

Ring

Slide lock

Numbered slots

Needle handle

Handle channel

Locking burr

Interchangeable needle tube

Slide-lock pushes down to lock needle in place.

Locking burr twisted into slot

Handle channel

Punch needle assembled

To assemble, insert the needle tube, locking-burr end first, through the handle channel until the tip is opposite the required slot. Twist the tip into the slot. Slide the lock down until firm contact is made with the tube.

The beauty of the speed needle is not only its speed—it will literally go as fast as you can turn the handle—but also its ability to hook materials and fibers that can't be used with other hooking tools. In contrast to the punch needle's preference for simple yarns (it refuses to work with knotty, slippery or fine yarns or multiple strands of yarn), the speed needle will hook anything you can thread through its eye. This includes unusual materials like wire, paper, plastics, fine sewing threads, monofilaments and multiple strands of yarn. Nearly everything except heavy rug yarns and even heavier wool-blanket strips can be used with the speed needle. Another advantage of this needle is that it will hook fiber strips as short as 2 in. long, whereas the punch needle needs a minimum 12-in. length to work well.

A misconception about the speed needle, which probably stems from its name, is that it's difficult to control. In fact, the speed needle is controlled by the turn of the handle and will operate at whatever pace you like.

Both needles are easy to use and can be mastered by anyone with a few hours of practice. Although I have based most of my work on these two tools, I wouldn't discourage anyone from trying any of the other hooking needles available. Explore what each tool has to offer. As you'll see, there are few rules that cannot be broken.

Working with the punch needle

Assembling the punch needle is an easy task. With the open channel facing you, insert one of the needles so the small locking burr at the end is lined up pto fit in the channel. Push the needle up into the handle until it's opposite one of the ten slots. The more needle you have sticking out, the longer the loops will be. Twist the needle until the locking burr fits into the slot. Push the slide lock down to hold the needle firmly in place. The tip of the slide lock will extend slightly over the needle when it's locked in place.

Thread the punch needle by holding it with the open channel up. Slip the yarn through the top ring (from the outside), then through the eye of the needle (from the inside). The yarn must ride inside the channel of the needle and handle. To seat it in the channel, push the yarn into the slot in the needle and hold the yarn firmly against the base of the handle with your left thumb. Then give a quick yank with your right hand to the yarn exiting the ring, and pull the strand back and forth until it runs freely through the channel. Pull the yarn through the needle tip until it extends about ½ in. beyond the eye of the needle.

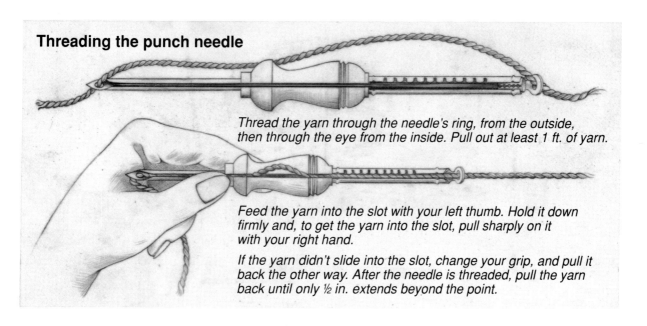

Threading the punch needle

Thread the yarn through the needle's ring, from the outside, then through the eye from the inside. Pull out at least 1 ft. of yarn.

Feed the yarn into the slot with your left thumb. Hold it down firmly and, to get the yarn into the slot, pull sharply on it with your right hand.

If the yarn didn't slide into the slot, change your grip, and pull it back the other way. After the needle is threaded, pull the yarn back until only ½ in. extends beyond the point.

Stitches are made with the punch needle by pushing the needle into the canvas as far as it will go, then bringing the needle back up just to the surface to keep the new stitch from pulling out. The needle is then inserted into the next hole to make the next stitch.

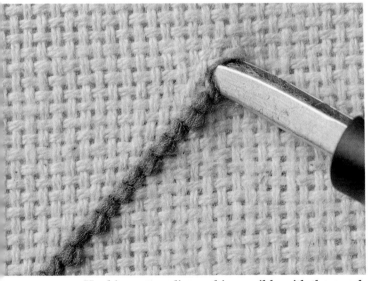

Hooking a true diagonal is possible with the punch needle, but it takes some practice. Each stitch is positioned in the backing one hole above and to the right (or left) of the previous stitch.

When you are learning to hook with the punch needle, it's best to start with the small needle, which requires less pressure and control. Set the needle in the No. 7 slot (for a medium-length loop), and begin with a four-ply knitting worsted yarn. Once you've threaded the needle, unwind an ample amount of yarn and place it near the work surface, so that you'll be able to hook with the yarn passing freely through the needle. If anything prevents the yarn from feeding freely, uneven loops will result.

With the backing material stretched as tightly as possible on the frame (see pp. 28-31), you're ready to begin hooking. Keep in mind that for the most part, you'll be hooking on the back of your design, with the wrong side facing you.

To begin hooking, first turn the stretched canvas to the wrong side and place the needle tip where you wish to start. Push the punch needle in as far as it will go and then bring it out slowly, stopping before you raise the tip past the surface. Bringing the punch needle out any farther will pull out the loop completely or make it uneven. At all times, the open slot of the needle will be facing up and the tip of the needle will be pointed in the direction of hooking. Move the needle along, pushing loops in every hole of the canvas, which will form even loops on the right side of the backing material. I like to keep my left hand on the back (working) side of the canvas, on top of and right next to the line of hooking, while my right hand holds the needle. This helps stabilize the backing and keeps it from moving up and down, which makes the hooking easier.

You can hook in any direction with the punch needle—up, down, backward, forward, even in circles—as long as the open slot is on top and the point of the needle is headed in the direction of hooking. It takes a bit more patience, however, to hook on a true diagonal. Since the backing material is a woven grid with only vertical and horizontal threads, you should be especially careful when attempting a diagonal line. The hooking must progress up one hole and over one hole of the backing with each stitch in order to produce even stitches. Work slowly, and don't be afraid to pull out any stitches that aren't correctly aligned. If you're off even one stitch, the line will quickly become noticeably crooked as it progresses.

To end a length of yarn or change colors, pull the needle just to the surface, then hold the yarn against the canvas with your finger and pull the needle away. Cut the yarn end flat with the surface of the canvas, and, with the point of the scissors, poke the cut end through to the right side of the work. If you want to follow strictly traditional methods, cut all such short ends flat to the surface (including the yarn tails where you've begun a row), and poke them through to the finished side so that they become part of the finished pile. The latex backing I apply during the finishing process (see pp. 112-113) holds the loops well, however, and prevents them from pulling out, so you needn't bother with poking all the ends to the right side.

If the needle becomes loose in its handle and slips while you're hooking, expand the upper channel of the needle. Do this by pushing the tip of a screwdriver into the channel and gently prying it open. This increases the needle's diameter and makes it fit tightly in the handle. If you find the needle is too tight, squeeze the upper channel of the needle with a pair of pliers. This reduces the needle's diameter, allowing the needle to slip in and out easily.

Altering the punch needle

I alter my hooking needles just as I do my materials, always searching for maximum effects. Some of my favorite punch-needle loops are ones that can't be made with the standard needle lengths. By making small alterations to the punch needle itself, it's possible to create very short or very long loops. If you want to make these adjustments on your needle, you may want to buy two needles, one for special loops and the other for regular use. Otherwise, you'll constantly be slipping the slide lock in and out or bending needles to fit. The cost of the punch needle is very reasonable, so it's worth having several on hand.

To create two shorter stitches with the punch needle, I've added two small notches to the needle shaft. I call these new slots No. 11 and No. 12, since the handle of the punch needle has ten slots ranging from longest to shortest loops, numbered 1 to 10. These new No. 11 and No. 12 stitches are very short loops, resembling needlepoint or petit point. I use them for outlining, flat backgrounds

To end a row or change colors with the punch needle, pull the needle to the surface and hold the yarn against the backing with your finger. Clip the yarn and push it to the right side of the canvas with the tip of your scissors, where it will be clipped later, if necessary.

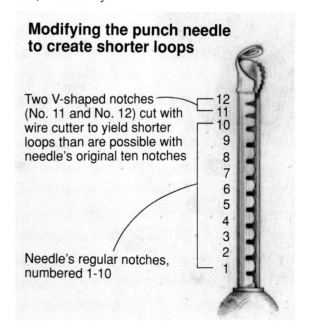

Modifying the punch needle to create shorter loops

Two V-shaped notches (No. 11 and No. 12) cut with wire cutter to yield shorter loops than are possible with needle's original ten notches

Needle's regular notches, numbered 1-10

12
11
10
9
8
7
6
5
4
3
2
1

or low relief in dimensional work. I use the medium and long loops produced by most of the regular slots of the needle for shag or sculpted forms. Combining these various stitches serves both functional and decorative needs.

To make these notches on your punch needle, first remove the slide lock by pushing it up and out the handle. With small tin snips or a wire cutter, cut two small V-shaped notches above the No. 10 notch, spacing them ⅛ in. apart like the other notches. You may have to bend the notches with a pair of small needle-nosed pliers to hold the locking burr and needle in place, because the slide lock remains permanently out of the needle channel when in the No. 11 and No. 12 positions.

A way to make shorter stitches without adding the V-cuts is to slide a common rubber washer over the punch needle's point, as shown in the photo at left. The washer acts as a bumper, preventing the needle point from extending farther into the canvas, which results in a shorter stitch. This is a simpler approach and works as well as making V-cuts, but it's a bit more inconvenient because the washer needs to be slipped on and off each time you change colors or end a row.

Once I'd discovered the effects I could get with shorter loops, I was eager to try making loops longer than the No. 1 setting allowed. I was able to do this by expanding the needle shaft so it held firmly in the lowest part of the handle, well below the No. 1 notch. This extended the loop lengths to 1¼ in. or more. To alter your needle, gently force

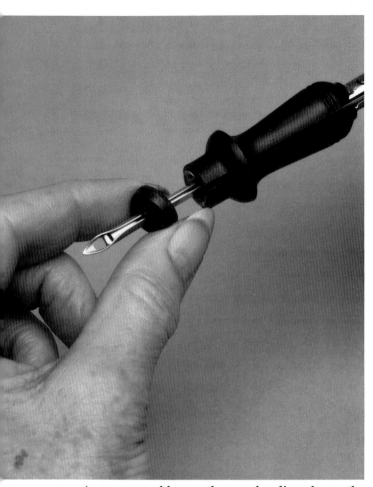

A common rubber washer can be slipped over the punch needle to create shorter stitches. The washer prevents the needle point from extending fully into the canvas, resulting in a shorter loop.

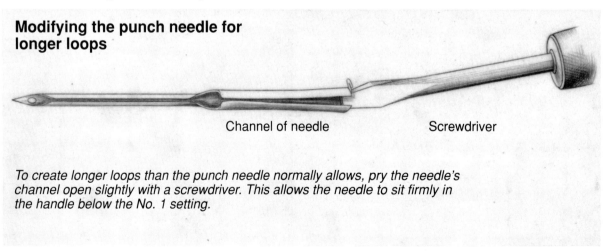

Modifying the punch needle for longer loops

Channel of needle   Screwdriver

To create longer loops than the punch needle normally allows, pry the needle's channel open slightly with a screwdriver. This allows the needle to sit firmly in the handle below the No. 1 setting.

the channel open with the tip of a screwdriver, as shown in the drawing on the facing page. The enlarged neck of the needle prevents it from moving up or down in the handle, even though it's not locked in place by the locking burr. With this adjustment, you can get a range of about four different settings. If you intend to use this approach regularly, an extra set of needles is a good investment, in order to save time.

To make even longer loops, you can use another technique. This method is possible, however, only if you're able to hook with one hand and reach around to the other side of the canvas with the other hand—in other words, you won't be able to do this if you're working with a large frame. To work this technique, shown in the drawing at right, set the punch needle to the longest loop and push the needle through the backing as far as it will go. Holding the yarn with the other hand, pull the needle back as usual while holding onto the loop. This will make a loop about 2 in. long.

If you want still longer loops, push the needle in, and, with the nonhooking hand held behind the canvas, pull the yarn from the needle out to any length you like. By consistently holding the yarn in a steady position and pulling it out uniformly, you can produce very even, long loops of up to 5 in. or 6 in. This technique is used for adding fringe or any decorative long loops.

Common punch-needle problems and solutions

Beginners frequently encounter problems with the punch needle. Most of the time the solutions are obvious. At other times it takes some investigating to find the answer. Below is a list of the problems you may run into and their solutions:

- Are the loops of different lengths? If so, it's likely that you're not pushing the needle into the backing far enough when making a loop, or that you're lifting the needle too far past the backing surface when starting to make the next stitch. Another cause might be that the backing is not stretched tightly enough, or that your yarn has caught on something and is not slack enough. You might be sitting on it, or it might be caught on the corner of the frame.
- Does your needle move around and come out of its notch? Check to see if the locking burr on the

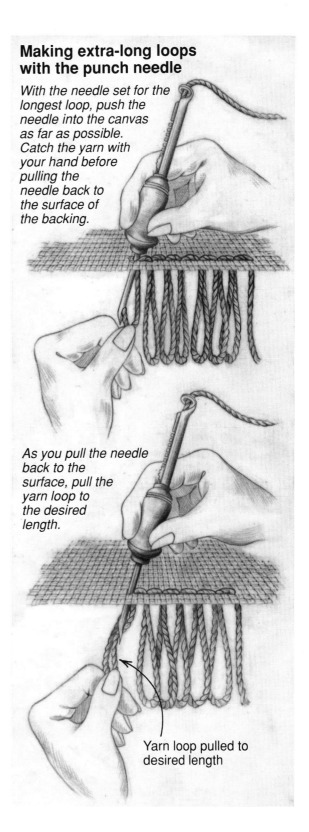

Making extra-long loops with the punch needle

With the needle set for the longest loop, push the needle into the canvas as far as possible. Catch the yarn with your hand before pulling the needle back to the surface of the backing.

As you pull the needle back to the surface, pull the yarn loop to the desired length.

Yarn loop pulled to desired length

needle top is pushed into the notch as far as possible. Also look to see if the slide lock is pushed down and over the needle far enough.

- Does the tip of your needle catch on the fiber? A likely cause is that the needle's tip is no longer smooth, probably because it has been dropped. Smooth any rough spots with an emery board or fine metal file.

- Does the needle slip out of the handle too easily? If so, gently force the slot open with a screwdriver to enlarge the channel. If the slot is too wide and it's difficult to push the needle in the handle, squeeze it lightly with a pair of pliers near the locking-burr end.

- Have the threads of the backing material gotten out of line from pulling out previous rows or from practice stitching? This can be corrected easily by using a heavy pin and briskly scratching back and forth over the fabric's surface, nudging the threads back into place. Be gentle if you're working on a weak backing material like burlap, which has threads that can break easily. It's often a good idea to apply a light wash of diluted adhesive over this area of the backing to strengthen the fibers before attempting to realign the threads (see also p. 113).

- Have you broken the ring end of the needle? The ring end, where the yarn passes through first, is the weakest area of the punch needle. It can be repaired by soldering. If the ring is bent but not yet broken, you may wish to add a bit of solder to the bend before it breaks.

The punch needle is a versatile tool. After you have become comfortable using it and your loops are nice and even, experiment to see how many different types of stitches you can produce. Try each of the ten different lengths. Work stitches very close together and also far apart. See what happens when the rows of loops are spaced close together and then farther apart. Work from top to bottom, and then from side to side. Practice going in circles.

Unlike other fiber work, hooking pulls out more easily than it goes in. So don't be afraid to experiment. You have nothing to lose. Try it all, then pull it out. Then try it again. The yarn can be used over again as long as it isn't cut, and the only judge of whether the hooking is good or bad is you.

Working with the speed needle

I enjoy using the speed needle immensely, and I hope everyone will consider trying it. As I mentioned earlier, the name may scare you into thinking it will go so fast that it will be uncontrollable. In fact, it works just like an eggbeater and goes only as fast as you turn the handle. For many years, I used my speed needle only for background work and large areas, before realizing how fast and versatile it could be for all hooking. Now I use the speed needle for 90% of my work, and I find it as easy to control as the punch needle.

The speed needle is easy to use. For your first attempt, you might want to begin with a medium-weight yarn like knitting worsted. Thread the yarn through the ¼-in. yarn guide, then down the shaft and through the eye of the needle. Using a pointed tool like a blunt pin or a darning needle, push the yarn through the needle's eye (or a fine looped wire may be used to pull the yarn through the needle). The yarn needs to extend only ½ in. past the end of the needle to start hooking.

The speed needle's five different loop lengths, ranging from ⅛ in. to ¾ in., are created by positioning the setscrew in one of the bellcrank's five holes. For short loops, place the setscrew in the first or second hole from the bellcrank's axis. For longer loops, use one of the other holes. If the screw is too tight to remove with your fingers, use the Allen wrench enclosed with the tool to loosen it. After you've made your adjustments, tightening the screw with your fingers is usually sufficient to hold it in place.

As with the punch needle, most of the hooking with the speed needle will be done on the wrong side of the finished piece. The tighter the backing fabric is stretched, the easier and the more successful the hooking will be. Keep plenty of slack yarn unwound near the work surface so that the yarn can pass through the needle freely. You'll constantly be pulling yarn from the skein to keep an unrestricted flow of yarn going through the needle as you work.

To operate the speed needle, place the point of the needle where you want to begin. Turning the

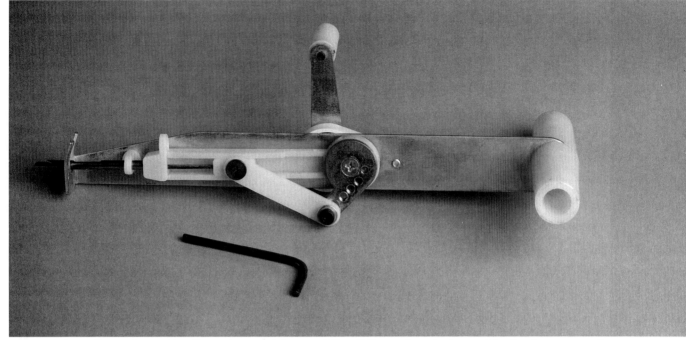

The speed needle can be easily adjusted to work loops of five different lengths by positioning its setscrew in one of five holes on the bellcrank of the needle shank. The screw is tightened either by hand or with an Allen wrench.

The speed needle and its use

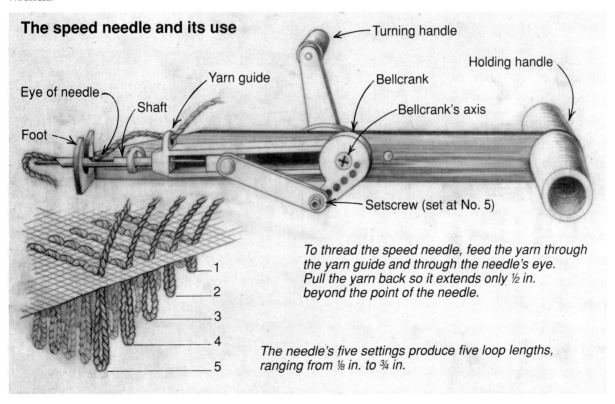

Turning handle

Holding handle

Yarn guide

Bellcrank

Eye of needle

Shaft

Bellcrank's axis

Foot

Setscrew (set at No. 5)

1
2
3
4
5

To thread the speed needle, feed the yarn through the yarn guide and through the needle's eye. Pull the yarn back so it extends only ½ in. beyond the point of the needle.

The needle's five settings produce five loop lengths, ranging from ⅛ in. to ¾ in.

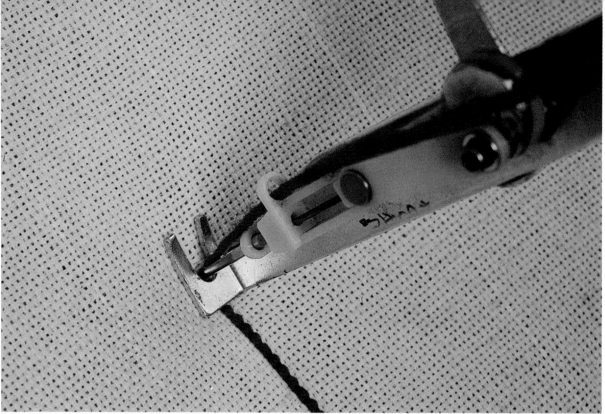

The speed needle operates like an eggbeater by turning its crank handle. To produce even stitches, it's important to hold the tool perpendicular to the backing surface, as shown in these photos, and to proceed at an even speed with firm pressure.

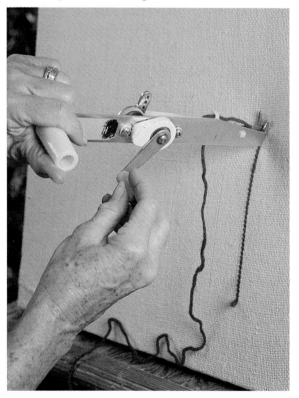

handle moves the needle forward on the canvas and produces stitches. Hold the speed needle perpendicular to the surface and maintain an even speed and firm pressure for uniform loops. It's also important not to go too slowly. You don't need to race, but a moderate pace will help you maintain even stitches, especially when you're following straight lines.

The speed needle will operate in any direction, as long as the point of the needle is headed in the desired direction. You can hook up and down, back and forth, in circles or on the diagonal. You can vary the density of the stitches to accommodate different weaves of backing material by slightly tilting the speed needle forward or backward. A slight tilt forward makes the stitches closer together; a slight backward tilt places them farther apart.

Turning or changing directions with the speed needle is also easy, since it's as natural to crank the tool's handle with the left hand as it is with the right. Simply leave the point of the needle in place, then turn the tool in any direction and resume your hooking.

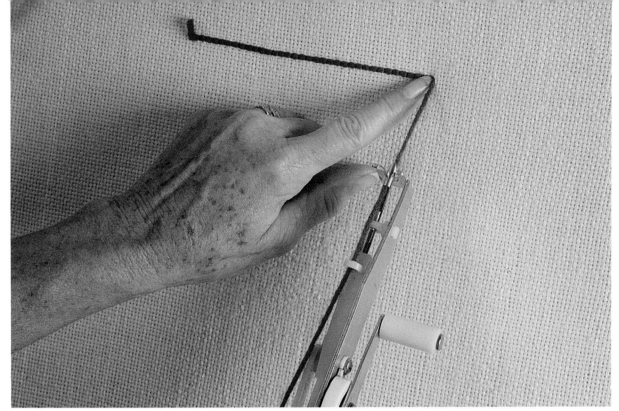

To change a color or end a row using the speed needle, place your finger on the end of the yarn as the needle comes to the surface. Clip the yarn and push it through to the other side of the canvas, where it will later be clipped, if necessary.

Changing a color or ending a row with the speed needle is similar to the procedure used with the punch needle. As the needle comes to the surface, hold the yarn with your finger. Clip the end and, with the scissors, push it through to the right side of the canvas. This strand will be trimmed later (see p. 112).

Once you get the feel of the speed needle, try all five loop positions to see the differences they create. Try a loop in each hole of the backing, and then compare the effect you get by hooking in every other hole. Next try hooking every row of the backing, then skip to every other row. How about skipping three rows? Each sequence gives a different texture when created with different yarns and lengths of loops. It becomes exciting to experiment with the possibilities.

I often draw with the speed needle, making lines on the backing and testing out designs. If they prove to be unsatisfactory, out they come. As with the punch needle, any work you don't like is easily pulled out. If the yarn hasn't been cut, it can be reused.

Common speed-needle problems and solutions

Although the speed needle is an easy tool to use, you may encounter some difficulties as you learn to use it. Below are some common problems and suggested solutions:

- Are your loops of different lengths? If so, you're probably not pressing firmly enough on the backing material, or your backing material may not be stretched taut enough. Another reason may be that your yarn is not slack enough or is catching on something.
- Are the backing fibers breaking or splitting? The needle point may not be entering the holes of the canvas correctly. Tilt the needle slightly forward or back so the needle point enters every hole easily.
- Does the setscrew keep falling out? If so, it's not screwed in tightly enough. It's best to hand-tighten this screw to prevent stripping the screw threads. If the problem continues, tighten it with the Allen wrench—but do so gently to protect the threads.

• Does the yarn fray when pulled backward through the needle? Sometimes the inside of the needle eye catches the fibers. To solve this problem, turn the needle upside down and pull the yarn out and then back again. Also, try pulling the yarn back and forth with tension on it. Some yarns, like those with nubby or fuzzy textures, can be just plain stubborn, but if you persist, they'll work.

I prefer the speed needle for almost everything, especially when I'm standing to work on large frames, because it's easy to manipulate and hooks quickly. But I also enjoy working with it on small lap frames. At first you may find it a bit awkward to work with this needle in a sitting position, but you will soon see how productive the speed needle can be. (See also the sidebar on working positions on pp. 77-79.)

Other commonly available tools and materials that will help you in hooking include (clockwise from top right) a matte knife; a marking pen; a tape measure; assorted pins, thumbtacks, needles and pushpins; a single-edged razor blade for slitting seams; a small screwdriver for removing thumbtacks; a crochet hook; a small embroidery shears; a large straight scissors; a pinking shears; a ruler; and masking tape.

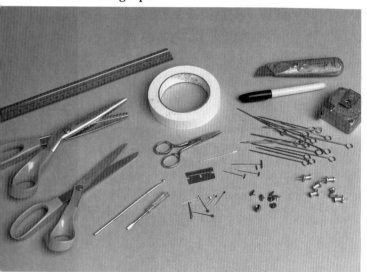

Other equipment

A selection of accessory tools, often those used in other fiber work, will help you in your rug hooking. A large and a small pair of scissors are necessary. The large pair should have blades 8 in. to 10 in. long, which are good for general-purpose cutting and trimming. I like scissors with plastic handles because they're easy on my hands. The smaller pair of scissors should be embroidery shears with blades 4 in. to 5 in. long. This pair is used for detail work and finish trimming. The quality of your work depends a lot on these shears, so select good ones, with strong, sharp points. Other types of scissors, such as pinking shears, are also often used to cut yardage to prevent raveling or to give an unusual texture to the cut strips.

You'll also need T-pins or other long-needled pins to help you keep yarn or backing material in place during your hooking. Some time ago I discovered upholstery pins, which have very long shafts and are very handy for pinning back excess backing material. They can be hard to find these days, but they're worth the search. Pushpins are frequently used to keep backing material in place when working on pieces larger than the frame (see pp. 106-109). Be sure to buy the ones with the extra long shafts and metal heads, since they are pounded into the wood with a hammer and the plastic heads shatter immediately.

I also keep a small screwdriver handy to remove thumbtacks from frames and a small crochet hook to help me work extremely tiny loops. A single-edged razor blade is useful for ripping seams of pieced backing material, and a matte knife comes in handy for cutting cardboard or Foam Core. Masking tape and marking pens are helpful for making paper patterns during the design stage of a project. The masking tape can also be used to control raveling. Finally, I keep on hand a variety of measuring devices—rulers, tape measures and yardsticks—so that I can check my accuracy as my work progresses.

Exploring rug-hooking techniques and materials

The basic stitches of the punch needle and the speed needle form the foundation for most of my hooking variations. At first, these stitches may seem to be very limited, but they offer endless possibilities once you start experimenting. Even the most common yarns can take on different personalities when hooked in short, medium or long loops. You'll find interesting contrasts between cut and uncut yarns. Experimenting with the many novelty yarns — such as mohair, bouclé and chenille — will also give unusual effects.

Although many rug hookers have created wonderful works using very basic stitches and yarns, I enjoy the endless discoveries that come from trying new techniques and unusual materials. Once you have mastered the basic stitches with the punch needle and the speed needle, try experimenting with some different materials to give your work a sense of uniqueness and individuality.

What materials should you use? In a word, everything. The problem is not that there are too few possibilities, but rather too many possibilities. With such a wealth of materials to choose from, the most difficult decision comes from having too many options. Add to this the many varieties of yarns, the endless selections in yardage and the possibilities of putting all these combinations together, and it can become overwhelming. I can spend nearly as much time trying to decide which of the ten blue fibers or fabrics to use as I do in actually hooking the piece. But what a nice problem. It was precisely this situation — having so many varieties on hand — that started me on the hooked variations shown in this book.

Once you begin exploring all the possibilities, ideas burst forth each time you pick up a new fiber. No material is sacred, and even the most absurd is worth a try. The most common material can give the most unusual effect.

To simplify choices about materials, I use a standard process for making decisions. First I decide what to make (see also Chapter 3 on design). Then

Swatches of hooked yarns (top to bottom): A heavy rug yarn, a medium-weight rug yarn and four-ply knitting worsted show various textures possible when a given yarn is hooked at different heights. All samples were hooked in short, medium and long loops, with the right half of the medium and long loops cut to show the alternative texture.

Novelty yarns like mohair take on very different characteristics when hooked in short, medium and long loops.

Decisions about which colors and materials to use are often made by piling the many options on the floor to sort through them. Selections that don't fit in with the overall feeling of the work are discarded.

I select the colors and turn to my stockpile of materials to see what I have on hand. I group all the fabrics, yarns and other materials in piles on the floor according to color. This gives me a sense of color and texture and how the materials relate to each other. I can quickly see what pleases me, what should be thrown out or what I need to purchase. I have found that the most interesting textures often come from combining as many different fibers of a related color as possible.

At this point excitement really peaks, so take advantage of the adrenalin that's flowing and keep your mind wide open to even the most farfetched ideas that may pop in. This euphoria is the very reaction you need when anticipating any new and glorious work. I don't continue with any project unless I feel strongly about the materials and the possibilities. The hooking process can be a very long one, and you truly need to believe that this work is going to be absolutely fantastic before you ever begin. Otherwise you'll never make it through the slow stages of development when you're tired and discouraged, as I always become about midway through the project. By then, I have put so much energy and materials into this now "horrible" thing that I keep going just to finish it. By the time I rip a little and change things, the work starts to look good again. And by the time it's off the frame, I feel it's a masterpiece — although I must admit I have come to realize that this elation is often due to the accomplishment of getting the work completed, whether it turned out exactly as I had pictured it or not.

Using plied yarns and threads

As few as two or as many as twenty or more strands of fiber can be hooked together at one time, but only when using the speed needle. Any number or type of strands can be combined as long as they fit into the needle and flow freely for hooking. These can range from rug and novelty yarns to those as delicate as thread. The speed needle seems made for this plied operation because it is tolerant of unusual weights and thicknesses of yarns. By contrast, trying to hook plied yarns with the punch needle is usually very frustrating, since the threads often become snagged. But the punch needle can handle some plied yarns, so, as always, try it and see.

A simple setup to ply threads to be hooked with the speed needle is made by propping a metal or wooden rod between two stools, as shown at left. The spools of thread are lined up on the rod to feed freely to the needle. Several yards of thread are pulled off the spools and plied by slipping them through the hand with uniform tension, as shown at right. They are then gently piled on the floor to await hooking. It's important to keep a slack pile of plied threads as the hooking progresses to maintain unrestricted feeding to the needle.

To achieve even, uniformly plied strands, you can use mechanical plying equipment, operated either by hand or electrically. These plying machines twist each strand uniformly around the others, making them into one even yarn. You can also use a spinning wheel, which plies nicely. The other option is to have random plying, with individual fibers hooked at the same time but twisted only occasionally. I have a Yarn Twister that plies up to three strands together, but use it only when a very uniform twist is mandatory. The limitation of only three strands and my impatience at having to add this extra step to the hooking process mean that the Yarn Twister sits idle on the shelf most of the time.

For thread plying, I have improvised a setup that uses metal or wooden rods propped between the legs of my studio stools, as shown in the photos above. This setup is not fancy, but it gets the job done and keeps the threads from mixing into an impossible tangle.

When should you use plied strands? Try them for a change of color and texture, to blend fine yarns for a heavier pile or to combine fine yarns too difficult to hook separately. Plying is a good way to recycle yarns that have been used for weaving, knitting or other hooking projects. The tighter twist produced by plying yarns on a yarn plier or a spinning wheel may also be desirable for rugs, especially ones that will get a lot of foot traffic.

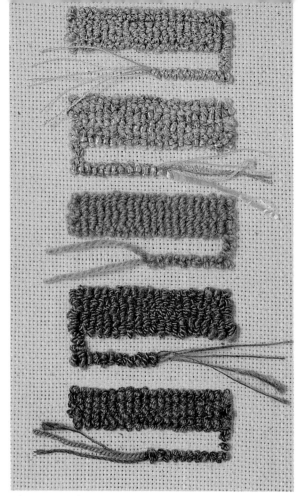

These examples of plied strands were all hooked on the shortest loop length. They show the range of subtle textures and colors available by mixing individual yarns. From top to bottom are: identical strands of linen; a mix of synthetic raffia, bouclé, wool, rayon and chenille; two-ply rug wool; rayon bouclé; and a mix of two-ply synthetic, bouclé and cotton yarns.

Four-ply strands of sewing thread in shades of blue hooked in long loops delicately contrast with the white background of four-ply knitting worsted hooked in short loops.

Hooking many strands of the same fiber is often the way I approach plying. One of my favorite finds is a shiny, black, very strong synthetic. It's very fine, almost like sewing thread, and one strand would hardly show in a hooked piece. When I combine 14 strands, the result is fantastic. But you must be armed with patience to avoid tangling the 14 individual threads that must be unwound from the main cone.

I might also ply a combination of different fibers all in the same color. A typical plied combination of whites might include a soft chenille, two crochet cottons, a shiny synthetic raffia and a satin bouclé. Plied together with the heavier whites, the finer threads acquire a presence they would lack by themselves. You can imagine the advantage this technique offers when you want to use up small amounts of mundane fibers left over from other projects.

Plying two or more lightweight yarns to create a heavier pile is another option. Often you'll find a good buy on rug yarn, but it's never the right color or the correct weight. If you ply this yarn with another, you can add interesting color and texture and at the same time produce a yarn with a thicker pile, which might serve for a wearable work if you desire.

I discovered some of the most unusual and surprising effects when I started hooking sewing threads with the speed needle. It sounds so impossible that for a long time I didn't even think of trying to ply thread. But my curiosity won out. I was amazed when I saw the first results, mostly because the fibers looked so soft, yet were sturdy and stiff. The trick is to coat the fine threads, once they're hooked, with a layer of diluted glue that acts as a stiffener and sizing material. The finished hooked threads retain their delicate appearance, yet are protected and stable.

To hook a project with plied threads, take several strands of any fine thread, from sewing to crochet weight. With your speed needle set to make either short or long loops, hook these threads after all of the other hooking and clipping have been completed on your piece. The threads are so soft that they will flop over, so you have to keep the hooking frame in a horizontal position. This will allow the soft thread to hang down on the underside of the canvas.

After hooking, place the finished canvas in a horizontal position, propped up on sawhorses, stools or table edges, with a plastic sheet on the floor under the work. Carefully brush a diluted solution of white glue over the threads from the back (working side) of the canvas. The solution is made by mixing ten parts of water to one part of white glue. Continue adding the glue solution until it saturates the backing and thread and drips through onto the plastic sheet below. Leave the work untouched and the frame in the horizontal position until the glue is thoroughly dry, usually overnight. When the work is dry, you can handle it normally, and you will see how stable the threads have become. In testing, I have found that the threads stay stiff even when washed, and they remain impervious to soiling. I do, however, pack work with such plied thread carefully when shipping it, and avoid rolling it tightly or placing it under excessive weight, which could crush the threads.

A variation on this finishing technique is to apply a water-soluble paint (acrylic) to the watered-down glue solution. Colors and textures mix as the solution runs through the threads, with each different fiber accepting the colors and the glue in varying degrees. Imagine white threads washed with a pastel mixture — how wonderful! Let your imagination take it from here.

Using cut yardage strips

If ever I thought I was getting bored with hooking, all I would have to do is look at yardage. In my former sewing days, I used to visualize all the glamorous outfits that could be made. Now I have only to see a ¼-in. strip and I go wild. I haven't tired of yarn for a minute, and the unpredictability of hooked fabric fascinates me even more. But the combination of yarn and cut yardage is the best of both worlds.

My rule of thumb with cut yardage is that any fabric strip, no matter what its fiber content, can be used if it can be threaded through the hooking needle and hooked without breaking. Yardage that ravels easily should be cut on the bias, although a straight cut on the grain will yield the strongest strip. (See p. 9 for a full explanation of cuts and the effects of grain.) Heavy fabrics, like sailcloth, do not hook as well as lighter-weight fabrics, because their stiffness prevents them from flowing easily through the needles. Be sure to join the cut-cloth strips with adhesive to create long strips before you begin hooking, or you'll spend all your time threading needles (see pp. 11-12 for joining instructions).

Wool   I don't think I've ever met a wool I didn't like. As far as I'm concerned, it's the perfect choice. Wool looks good, feels great and dyes and wears well.

For cut strips of wool, a firm weave is necessary since most strips will be ¼ in. wide or less. Wool strips should be cut on the straight of the material for maximum strength, or they may pull apart when hooked. It's always a good idea to cut a short strip in different widths to test for strength before cutting into your entire supply of fabric. As mentioned earlier, changing the width of the strip by a mere ¹⁄₃₂ in. can make the difference in whether it pulls apart or whether it works in the hooking needle.

Good wool blankets have been my favorite background material for years. Army & Navy sur-

A diluted white-glue solution is brushed onto the back of the canvas where plied threads have been hooked. The glue drips through the backing, saturating the threads, which, when dry, remain upright, stiff and protected from soiling.

Each square was hooked with ¼-in. strips in short, medium and long loops. Clockwise from top left: cross-grain velour, pulled into cord (on left) and hooked flat (on right); straight-grain organdy strips (on left) and medium-weight wool (on right); bias-cut cotton (on left) and satin (on right); and bias-cut plain cotton (on left) and printed cotton (on right).

Cut yardage strips, all ¼ in. wide, can be used in unlikely ways. Clockwise from top left: straight-grain satin, which produces a soft, thready texture; cross-grain terry cloth and cross-grain suede cloth, stretched into cords; and straight-grain wool hooked at the bottom of the square with an even loop and at the top with a random-length loop.

plus stores are unsurpassed for the quality and price of their blankets. I often dye these blankets haphazardly, not stirring the dye mix, which gives me nice variegated colors. After dyeing the blankets, I tear the fabric in 1-in. strips, then cut these lengths into ⁷⁄₃₂-in. strips with the cloth stripper. The torn edge adds a nice softness to the otherwise crisp, cut edge. It may seem foolish, but I've even raveled one or two threads off these heavy blanket strips just to take advantage of the softer look and texture the raveled edge offers.

As much as I dislike ripping up clothing, I'll do so for a good-quality wool. If you're using old clothing, make sure you start with cleaned and pressed fabric, because it's unnecessarily difficult — if not impossible — to clean and press all the cut strips. Also, remove all machine stitching and any sewing threads since they'll be very noticeable once the strips are hooked.

Cottons and cotton blends Cotton fabrics are a delight to work with, especially the prints. Even though I've worked with cotton prints for many years, I still love seeing how different a print looks when it's hooked. Some of the worst patterns, which you'd never dream of wearing, become great successes when cut and hooked. I use plain fabrics just as often as printed ones, since they come in a nice array of textures and a wide range of colors. When you consider the results, it's a shame so few people use cottons for rug hooking.

Cutting cotton strips can be a challenge, because the cloth stripper sometimes has trouble with lightweight materials. But with a little persistence, you can make it perform for you. You may have to cut several rows, adjusting and readjusting the tension on the cutter wheel to get it to cut correctly. Again, test a short ¼-in. wide strip, pulling it to see if it's strong enough to be hooked. With cotton

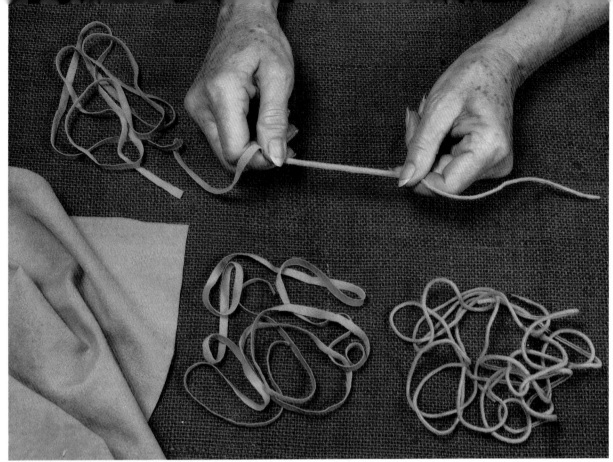

To make cording from flat, ¼-in.-wide strips of velour cut on the cross grain, simply pull the strip taut. Pull 6-in. sections of the longer strip at a time, until the entire length has been corded.

or other lightweight materials, I suggest cutting the strips on the bias, since they will ravel badly if they're cut on the straight grain.

Satins My obsession with shiny, reflective materials will never cease. I find satin to be a very special fabric, but because it ravels so easily, I always try to cut it on the bias in ¼-in. widths. This may be a little wider than you would cut other fabrics, but, with satin, this width is needed for strength.

You may discover a few satins that aren't strong enough to work well when cut on the bias. Cut these on the cross grain or straight grain and save them for use when you want a more threadlike look. Always hook satin with a punch needle, since the speed needle often folds the strip, producing an unattractive effect.

Velours Velour is one material I buy in quantity. You only need to hook with it once to get completely carried away. Imagine how great it would look next to a soft wool, a shiny satin or a flat yarn. No matter where you put it, it always looks good.

The best thing about velour is that it's very forgiving in the way it's cut and handled. For the best results, try cutting it on either the length or the width of the fabric, rather than on the bias. For a clean ¼-in. velvet-ribbon look, cut on the length of the velour.

One of my favorite effects is velour cording that ·is made from strips cut on the cross grain. To produce this cording, cut a ¼-in. strip and pull it hard on each end. Your ¼-in. straight strip will automatically turn into a gorgeous round velour cord, with velvet edges and no harsh ravels. When I hit upon this remarkable technique, I thought I had died and gone to heaven. A ¼-in. strip that has been pulled into cording works best in the speed needle and can be used at almost any loop length. If you decide to leave the straight-cut velour strip flat and unpulled, it will hook into handsome ribbonlike loops.

Velvets and silks After such success with velour, I was disappointed in velvet. It is such a beautiful fabric, but, when cut, it often ravels; unfortunately, it cannot be cut on the bias to prevent this raveling. If I have some velvet on hand, I experiment before going to the trouble of cutting all the strips, only to be discouraged with the results. Sometimes I come across a piece of velvet that's too irresistible to pass up. Then I force it to work, but this often means hooking slowly, which is very tedious.

Silk is so precious that I don't use it very often. When I do, I make certain it's played up to its best advantage by using it in a key area or as a focal point of a design. I always try to cut silk on the bias to avoid fraying, but this isn't always possible. If I really want to use the silk, I don't worry about raveling.

Knits Knits are another material I buy in quantity. Wait until you see the remarkable change in this fabric when it's stretched and pulled. The edges curl, forming a rolled, cordlike strip. The fabric really comes alive.

To produce cords, cut a ¼-in. strip across the width of the fabric (it rarely stretches into a rolled length when cut on the straight grain). Each knit is so different that I can never predict the texture without cutting a strip and pulling it. But I do know that this technique can turn an ugly polyester into a great texture. An especially nice contrast is produced by combining the stretched fabric cording with unstretched flat strips.

Terry cloth, especially the knitted variety, creates another exciting texture when hooked. It looks terrible when first cut in strips, but it pulls into a nice cord. This material leaves a big mess, so expect a big cleanup of fuzzballs after stretching the strips. The nice thing about this stretching technique is that you often double or triple the length of each strip. I stretch only a few yards at a time, while hooking, for even consistency.

Another nice thing about stretched knits is that they often resemble commercial cording and ribbon, which hook beautifully but cost dearly. When you are in doubt about whether to buy a particular color of commercial cording or ribbon, try the pulled-knit technique with the same color of terry cloth first.

Using reflective materials

Once you start exploring nontraditional materials for your hooking projects, you will never look at another material in the same way. After I got over the purist notion of using only fiber in my work, I started looking with fascination at all the possibilities of combining mixed elements. I have always been attracted to anything shiny, liking both the bold statement a reflective surface makes alone and the way it makes neighboring textures come alive. When I started using reflective materials in my hooking, it was an exciting breakthrough. I found that materials like metal wire, washers, Mylar, plastics, monofilament and foils can add a whole new dimension to the work.

Metals Wire, washers, springs, grommets, eyelets, brads, nuts, foils — all these materials and more can be used in your hooking projects. I'm always looking for sources of these metals for my work. Surplus stores and salvage yards are two of the best sources because they have such an unusual selection and usually sell metal inexpensively in bulk. And while you're there, you're bound to find other unknowns you've never considered including in your work.

Near Seattle, not too far from where I live, we have the Boeing Surplus Warehouse, which is filled with a huge array of salvage materials. Each trip is an adventure. It's not unusual for me to bring home two buckets of metal washers, all bought for a song. The frustration comes when you race back the next week to get more, and not a single one is left. But on that trip you discover a great roll of wire, which you have been hoping to find for the past year.

Of course, not everyone has access to a surplus store as intriguing as Boeing. But I have found that any salvage yard is worth investigating on a routine basis, since these yards have such an unusual array of metals and inexpensive bulk items. For small quantities of metal elements, the local hardware store is an alternative, but for large-scale works, it's too costly.

One of my favorite metals to use in hooked projects is wire. Many times in the past I've tried to use it, but failed because I didn't have the right kind of wire. It must be fine enough and flexible enough to hook well, and it works only with the

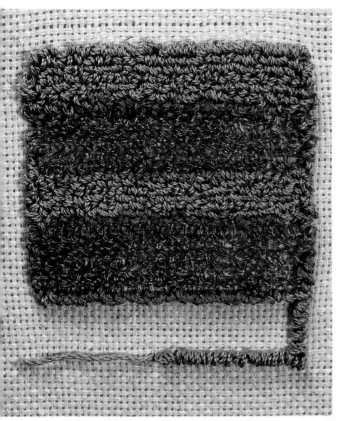

In this sample, a double strand of 20-gauge nickel-coated copper wire was hooked in low loops between bands of two-ply cotton, also hooked in low loops.

speed needle. I have found several types of wire that perform well, most around 24 gauge or finer. My favorite is a nickel-coated copper wire (silver in color), which I found at a surplus store. Fine copper wire from the hardware store also works well. Wires come in such great colors — silver, copper, brass, gold — that I generally decide on the color I want to use, then shop for the appropriate gauge needed for the project.

A double or triple strand of a wire hooked in a short speed-needle loop (No. 1 or 2) usually looks best. Longer loops of wire bend and lose their shape. When you hook with wire, the wire's stiffness forces open the weave of the backing fabric, which isn't particularly attractive. To close the weave, first secure the wire to the backing with adhesive. Do this immediately after hooking by running a continuous bead of household cement

over each row of wire on the back (wrong side) of the canvas. When this is dry, cover the whole area you've just glued with a strip of cotton sheeting, applied with a flexible adhesive like Tacky Glue. The combination of the household cement and the fabric strip will hold the wire securely in place.

In most cases, it's necessary to paint the backing under the wire loops in order to fill the holes and blend any sheeting fabric so it won't show. I prefer a water-soluble acrylic paint (available in all colors by the tube) in a matching color. Thin the paint enough so you can brush it on the front side of the canvas and cover the area under and around the wire. The paint will get on the wire, but it can be easily removed before it dries with a soft cloth or a Q-Tip worked between the rows of wires. Latex will later be spread over the entire back and will secure the wire, sheeting and hooking as one (see Chapter 4 for more information on finishing).

Metal elements can also be added to hooked work with adhesives, and it's amazing how well metal adheres to fiber. The trick is to find the appropriate adhesive and to use enough pressure to hold the metal elements down during drying time. The various finishes on shiny metals often determine which adhesive works best; you'll need to test to determine which one to use. Usually Super Tacky, Tacky Glue or a clear household cement bonds wonderfully. (For more on adhesives, see pp. 12-14.)

It's generally best to hook first and then add the metal elements, although in some pieces I have had more success by hooking after the metal parts mwere already on. Test both ways to see which works for you.

Metal washers provide a clean, geometric element in a hooked design, and they can often be painted in a wide range of colors. For a full description of how they are applied to a hooked project, see the photos on pp. 70-72.

Grommets, eyelets and rivets, which are available at most variety or fabric stores, also make interesting additions to hooked work. No adhesive is required to apply these elements, because they are assembled in two parts with interlocking prongs and usually come with their own setting instructions and tools. Care must be taken, however, to apply them correctly. I mark the exact spots where I want them to go, hook the back-

In this sample, a square of four-ply knitting worsted was pierced by three eyelets. Scattered around the sample are various eyelets, grommets and other metal elements that can be used for decorative effects in hooked projects.

ground and leave unhooked the small area for the metal element. This approach makes application easier if the hooked background becomes too heavy. If you're working with dense hooking on which you want to use eyelets but fear you'll have trouble attaching them, consider using grommets (large eyelets), which will normally accept a thicker background than their smaller cousins.

Metal springs are another element I often incorporate in my work. I think I use them so much just because they're fun to make. Some years ago I used springs to hold the heavy warp in several large commissioned window hangings at the Seattle-Tacoma Airport. The durability and uniqueness of this technique inspired me to add springs to later works, both woven and hooked. Since quite a few springs are usually incorporated into a piece, it's often easier and less expensive — and definitely more fun — to make your own.

Metal springs can easily be made from wire and offer unlikely additions to a hooked piece. They add an element of surprise and sometimes a nice reflective highlight.

Making springs is a simple procedure (see the photos at right). First, find a sturdy metal rod the diameter you want for your finished springs. An 8-in. to 12-in. rod is long enough to handle several springs at once. Select any wire you want, from very fine to very heavy gauge, and cut it into 10-in. to 12-in. lengths. Place the rod in a vise or a clamp that will hold it securely in a horizontal position. With pliers, hold one end of the wire firmly against the rod. With the other hand, wrap the wire evenly around the rod, keeping the wrapping as close together as possible. When the entire length of the wire has been wrapped around the rod, release the pliers and push the wire spring against the vise end to compact the spring and make it uniformly spaced. Remove the spring from the rod and pull it open to the length and stretch you want.

Make sure you wear gloves when making springs since the wire ends can "bite." For uniform springs, do the entire supply needed at one time. Measure the wire to exact lengths before wrapping it on the metal rod, and pull the spring tension equal on all of them.

When applying springs to your hooked piece, keep in mind that they pierce through the finished fiber easily. Bend the ends well into the backing to hold them. Additional cement on the back may be needed to hold them securely. I've also learned from past experience that springs are very tempting, especially in wall pieces in public spaces. Viewers cannot resist pulling them to see what they are. So expect to make replacements if your work is vulnerable to curious fingers.

Mylar, acrylics and plastics Modern technology has produced a wealth of fibers that rug hookers of just 50 years ago couldn't have begun to imagine. Some of the materials have emerged from advances in chemistry and the manufacture of synthetics, while others have resulted from the unusual fiber needs of our space-exploration program. These wondrous materials bring unique colors, textures and qualities to hooking. As the technology continues to develop, it's exciting to discover what new materials can be added to the hooking enthusiast's palette.

Mylar is a reflective material that I feel has never been explored fully by fiber workers. A metal-

Metal springs are made by wrapping 10-in. to 12-in. lengths of metal wire around a rod, whose diameter determines the spring's size. With the rod held in a vise, hold one end of the wire against the rod with pliers. Then wrap the wire evenly around the rod, using a sweeping circular motion, as shown at top. With the wrapping completed, make the spring uniform by compressing the wire against the vise. Remove the spring and stretch or curl it to the desired shape, as shown above.

Black knitting worsted and a double strand of ⅛-in. black Mylar were hooked in alternating rows in this sample.

ized polyester film developed for space rockets, Mylar has the look and durability of metal with the ease of fiber in its application. The most common variety of Mylar is the shiny silver, sold in widths ranging from 36 in. to 60 in. With luck, you can find Mylar in wonderful colors, usually in specialty or large art stores. I've found narrow widths (⅛ in. and less) by the cone in various colors at weaving-supply stores, which is fortunate since it is impractical to cut Mylar yardage into strips that narrow. I often combine Mylar with other fibers and fabrics, and it can produce striking effects. In one piece, a sample for which is shown in the photo above, I combined ⅛-in. black Mylar with two-ply wool. I've also found that alternating rows of flat black wool with the very shiny Mylar gives the appearance of beading.

I treat Mylar yardage the way that I treat fabric. It can be cut into strips and hooked, but the ends need special attention to secure them. Mylar rejects most adhesives, so you must use anything that will hold. Depending on the look, construction and function of your piece, this may mean a strong transparent tape, staples, machine stitching or household cement.

In addition to Mylar, I'm also fond of acrylics and plastics. They react with such brilliance to light that I never tire of using them, either alone or in combination with other fibers. I'm amazed that so few fiber artists have put these shiny, transparent materials to work for them. The moment a work becomes dreary or boring, I add a bit of shine, and it immediately perks up. I generally use the clear varieties, mostly because they are so readily available. Hardware, fabric and drapery stores carry different weights by the yard. I'm also constantly on the lookout for colored acrylics and vinyls used commercially and occasionally found in art specialty stores.

Many fiber textures are possible with acrylics and plastics, depending on how the yardage is cut. I like a pinked edge cut with pinking shears for a high shag (see pp. 59-65 for information on shag). You can also cut strips of any width down to ¼ in. quickly and easily, using either a paper cutter or scissors. The strips become very uniform if the yardage is folded many times, enabling you to cut up to ten strips at once. The acrylic sheets automatically stick together, making narrow cuts easy to do. These strips can be hooked if they're not too wide, and they give a wonderful texture.

The biggest challenge in working with acrylics is finding a way to join the slick, nonporous surfaces so that you can make long strips to hook. Each fabric reacts to adhesive differently, so test you must. If Tacky Glue or household cement doesn't hold, I occasionally resort to staples if I can conceal them or, alternatively, to a strong, clear tape. To secure the strips to the backing, I often knot the strips, which creates an interesting texture and provides a secure hold. Don't let this material discourage you—the results are worth the fuss. Also be sure to try stretching narrow strips. The strips take on a curly look with a whole new personality.

Metallic yarns and threads Metallic fibers have become popular recently for use in fiber work. Most are hooked like any other yarn or thread, and they usually perform best when hooked with the speed needle. Heavy metallic cords may need an improvised hooking technique, such as using a crochet hook. The main concern with these slippery fibers is keeping the loops in place—they

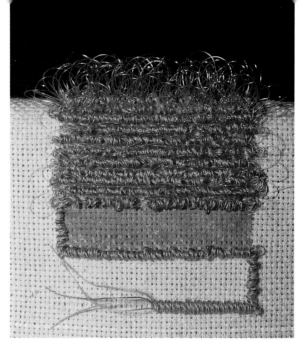

Five varieties of metallic threads were hooked amid a background of four-ply knitting worsted in this sample. Top to bottom: plied strands of fine Mylar, ⅛-in. strips of silver paper gift wrap, strands of twisted metallic yarn, a multi-strand of metallic and black twisted yarns, and heavy metallic cord.

Monofilament can produce unique results. In this square, which has a painted background, plied strands of two-tone cotton thread were hooked in short loops between rows of clear monofilament, hooked in medium-length loops in the lower half of the square and long loops at the top.

like to slide out with the slightest touch of the hand. With some especially slippery fibers, extra precaution must be taken to hold the loops in place, often immediately upon hooking one row or a small area. Tacky Glue or household cement must be applied from the back (working) side of the canvas, carefully covering only the metallic threads. A final coating of latex during the finishing stages normally holds all threads securely (see pp. 112-113).

With such a wide variety of metallic yarns and threads available, it may take some searching to find an appropriate type for hooking. If the materials are not available in local weaving shops, I turn to mail order. I also always give a glance when passing the gift wrap or mailing section of drug, variety and grocery stores, since they offer new surprises each season.

Monofilaments Monofilament, also known as fishing line, hooks into fascinating loops. At first you will think that this fine, hard-to-control material is just plain scary, and you'll never believe that it will work. But once you try it, you'll love the results. The longer loops form bows that

open up in the center, and since the monofilament is stiff, they stay in this unusual bow shape.

I was introduced to monofilament when a local sporting-goods store went out of business a few years ago. They had all this fishing line for sale at nearly giveaway prices. At the time, I was thinking of the possibilities of using the line for weaving, not hooking. But after experimenting with it, I began tmo use it in all sorts of new ways in my hooking projects.

The type I like best is the clear, transparent line. Some varieties come in opaque or dull white, others in greens and blues, but I feel none of these add much zip to hooked work because they lack the transparent, reflective qualities of the clear. My favorite gauges are the 10-lb. to 20-lb. test weights. Monofilament can be hooked in double or single strands, using speed-needle settings No. 2, No. 3 and occasionally No. 4.

As with wire or acrylics, hooking with monofilament takes special attention. It should be the last thing you hook, so that you can immediately control those slippery loops and keep them from going their own merry way. The cut ends in particular must be left long (½ in. or more) or they will fly

Natural raffia has an interesting dull texture and, like fabric, can be hooked, painted and dyed. This sample shows raffia hooked in short, medium and long loops, with half of the long loops cut.

Synthetic raffia mimics natural raffia in texture but is available in shiny, bright colors as well as black and white. Here it's shown hooked in short, medium and long loops.

Some gift-wrap ribbons create a crisp, shiny texture when hooked. In this sample, ¼-in. ribbon was split in half to produce ⅛-in. strips, which are hooked in short, medium and long loops.

This cloth ribbon automatically folded to half of its original width when hooked in short and medium loops but remained unfolded when hooked in the longest loops.

out. The moment one row is finished, I seal it on the back with household cement, letting the tube form a continuous bead of adhesive over the entire row.

As does wire, the stiff fishing line enlarges the holes in the backing material, which I find offensive. I use paint to cover and fill them, and if the holes become too open, I glue narrow cloth strips on the wrong side to hide them, just as I do with wire. Unlike with wire, however, I'm careful not to get paint on the fishing line, since its porous surface prevents removing the paint as easily as with wire.

Monofilament looks better if hooked in higher loops over a colored, low-hooked background. Since the monofilament is transparent, it needs a background of fiber or color to be effective.

If your low-hooked background is worked in an open pattern or with delicate materials like thread, you may want to consider painting the backing material. This should be done first, before the low background is hooked. For painting, I prefer to use a light wash of fabric paint or dye, such as Versatex, which I brush on like watercolor. When the backing dries, you can hook a low background of multi-strands of common sewing threads, crochet cotton, yarn or cut strips.

One of the best things about using monofilament is that it serves to protect the fragile threads or fibers hooked as the low background. In effect, the higher, stiff monofilament loops prevent fingers or soil from touching the lower ground. This technique has been a perfect solution for use on fiber works in public spaces, because it provides a protective coating to even the most delicate fibers and colors.

Good lighting plays an important role when displaying works containing monofilament. Without strong spotlights, the more delicate loops will hardly show. When used well, lighting gives the works a luminous quality that can resemble a surface covered with raindrops. I don't know of any other material that can give such a magical quality to hooked works.

Using raffia, paper and ribbon
In addition to yarn, thread, cut yardage and assorted metal elements, plant-based materials like raffia and paper offer interesting texture pos-

sibilities for hooking. Natural raffia, shown in the top left photo on the facing page, is a beige, grasslike fiber with a soft, dull texture. It hooks just like fabric, and dyes and paints well. It's an interesting material that can be used either alone or in combination with other fibers. Synthetic raffia, shown in the top right photo on the facing page, looks similar to its natural cousin but is made of polyesters and comes in wonderful soft pastels, as well as black and white. Because it's bright and glossy, synthetic raffia adds good contrast in a work. Both natural raffia and synthetic raffia come in ½-in. to 1-in. widths and are very durable and resistant to soil. White synthetic raffia is one of my favorite whites, especially when used in combination with other differently textured white materials.

If you have a paper cutter or a shredder, paper offers some unique textures when hooked. You will only be able to hook paper that has a good cotton fiber content, which is recognizable by its pliability and clothlike feel. Paper must be cut into thin strips of about ⅛ in. wide, or it will wrinkle. I've had great success using a crochet hook to form 1-in. to 2-in. cut and uncut loops.

Several finishes can be added to paper to make the strips more pliable and durable. These finishes include flexible acrylic sealants like those used in découpage. Experiment with adding finishes before or after hooking, depending upon the effect you want.

Ribbon, shown in the bottom photos on the facing page, is another obvious choice as a hooking material. It is available in almost limitless colors and a range of widths that answers almost any need. Both inexpensive gift-wrap ribbon and finer cloth ribbon hook well, and each produces a distinctive texture. Gift-wrap ribbon can easily be split in half from its original ¼-in. width to create ⅛-in. strips for hooking. Similarly, cloth ribbon will sometimes automatically fold in half when hooked in shorter loops, creating a narrower strip.

Making fabric shag
There are times when the texture you want just can't be obtained with the speed needle or punch needle. In such cases you may want to explore other ways of attaching the fabric to the backing. One approach is fabric shag, a nonhooked tech-

Fabric shag is created by poking squares of cut yardage through the backing canvas, leaving tufts of fabric to create a soft, high texture. The squares can be cut either with pinking shears for a decorative edge, as they are on the left, or with straight shears, as they are on the right.

nique that creates an explosion of texture and color on the canvas. Fabric shag is worked by cutting fabric into squares or circles and poking them through the backing. The tufts of fabric extending from the surface of the work create a shag texture unlike any that can be made with yarn.

I have to laugh when writing about this great technique. At first I really believed that I had invented the whole thing, and I felt like a genius. I thought I was the only one working with this unique texture. Then last year I started corresponding with a wonderful lady in Newfoundland, exchanging hooking ideas with her. I was so interested in Newfoundland's traditional "prodders" (hookers) that she sent me a volume of information and pictures of local work. As you've probably guessed, I found out that my invention

has been around for years, probably a century or more, and that it originated in England, where it is called "poking." I vary the technique a bit from the traditional approach—which pokes a continuous piece of fabric through the backing, a bit like rya weaving—but the resulting shag texture is the same. In spite of learning that I wasn't such a genius, I still love this technique and use it with great pleasure. I hope you do too.

I've developed two basic versions of fabric shag—high shag and low shag. In high shag, the fabric squares are poked and left uncut. In low shag, the squares are trimmed closer to the hooked surface, creating a shorter and denser pile than that of high shag.

The height of untrimmed high shag is determined primarily by the size of the fabric squares used. I like a 3-in. to 3½-in. square for most surfaces, but any size will work well. The thing that's critical with shag is to cut the material so that it doesn't ravel. Raveled edges look bad, they're difficult to repair and they don't wear well.

I've learned from experience to test a 3-in. square for raveling before cutting all the squares. First, try cutting a square on the straight grain with regular scissors and then pull the edges of the square to see how easily they fray. If there's a lot of fraying, try cutting an edge with pinking shears to see if that stops the raveling. If it doesn't, use a bias cut, which is almost guaranteed to prevent fraying.

A straight cut works well on firmly woven fabrics, cotton, knits, backed cloth and interlocks. A bias cut is a must for shag in floor rugs or any piece that will be used, worn or washed. It's also a must for shag made from wools with a soft nap, sheers and especially metallics, all of which will ravel forever. Nothing is more disappointing than seeing unwanted threads spreading across your work, knowing that you will eventually be losing most of them to the vacuum cleaner. On the other hand, the thready, raveled look can add a unique texture to a surface that's too flat, but this texture should be reserved for wall hangings. In such works, you can even exaggerate the thready look by brushing the surface briskly to form a soft, fuzzy pile.

Aside from the issue of raveling, you can cut the squares for shag with either regular shears or pinking shears, depending on the edge you prefer. A pinked edge not only helps prevent raveling but is also very decorative. I often combine the two edges to introduce a subtle difference.

For a slightly different shag, try cutting the fabric into circles, which produces a petal effect. Because you lose the points of the squares, you'll need to cut these circles larger than the squares. For example, a 4-in. to 4½-in. circle will generally produce the same shag height as a 3½-in. square. I usually cut these circles with regular scissors, since the even, straight edge looks nicer on these petals than a pinked edge.

A painted edge is another option for shag, whether made from fabric circles or squares. This adds another color dimension and introduces a crisp texture to an otherwise soft surface. On one

Using circles of fabric instead of squares to work shag creates a petal effect. The fabric circles can be cut with a straight edge (at top) or a pinked edge (at bottom). Painting the edges of the circles gives the shag another dimension of color as well as a crisp texture.

To make the circles, first trace them in pencil on the fabric, using a pattern or template like a plastic cup, and then apply a thin layer of acrylic paint to the edges. When the paint dries, cut out the circles and work them as shag.

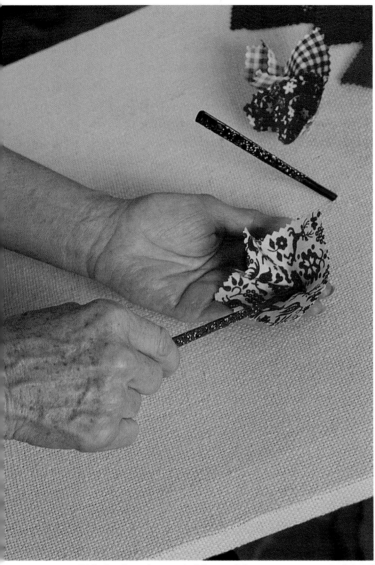

Fabric shag is created by poking squares or circles of cut yardage through the right side of the canvas backing with a pointed tool like a chopstick, as shown above. To work shag, make a hole in the canvas with the chopstick, leaving it in place temporarily. Then place the tip of a second chopstick in the center of the fabric square or circle and press into the fabric.

Remove the place-holder chopstick and poke the fabric and point of the tool in the empty hole, as shown above right. The material is forced in just enough to hold it, generally ¼ in. to ⅜ in.

The finished shag at right uses dozens of squares of fabric in related tones to create a subtle mix of color and texture.

wall hanging I wanted a field of color ranging from hot pink to orange, but I had only five shades of each in my scrap bag. By painting circles in shades of red, I got the intermediate tones I wanted. And the painted edges gave the cloth a nice stiffness and kept the circles from raveling.

Painting shag may sound laborious, but it isn't. Use a thinned water-soluble acrylic paint for a stiff edge, or a fabric dye like Versatex for a soft finish. Apply the paint to the fabric before cutting the squares or circles, using a cup or glass the diameter of the circle you want as a template. Slap the paint on fast, letting it add a watercolor-wash look to the fabric. Remember to test before painting all the circles, since the colors will look darker than they really are when the fabric's wet. When the paint is dry, iron out any wrinkles in the fabric, which will also heat-set the dye. Then cut the circles with regular shears, using a paper pattern.

More often than not, you'll be using scraps or odd-size remnants to cut shag pieces. If you can't cut the fabric on the bias yet don't want an edge that ravels, seal the edges with a diluted adhesive made from ten parts white glue to one part water. If you mark out a grid sized to the dimensions of the squares you want and apply the glue over the grid before cutting the fabric, you'll be able to seal the edges of two squares at once. When the fabric dries, cut the grid apart with pinking shears, which will further protect against raveling. This adhesive treatment works well on smooth fabrics, but it's not effective on materials with soft piles like wool, velvet or velour. For another interesting effect, try adding fabric or acrylic paint to the adhesive solution to produce colored edges.

Fabric shag is created with very simple tools. You can use any slightly pointed object to push the fabric through the backing or the hooked background. Don't go out and buy a special tool, just see what you have on hand. I have a favorite plastic chopstick that works beautifully. A tailor's stiletto or a tapestry bobbin also works well. A pencil, however, is not a good choice, because the lead is too pointed and will pierce the cloth. You can also improvise with a wooden dowel partially sharpened to a blunt point.

Unlike other techniques, most shag is worked from the front of the piece. To create the shag, first poke a hole in the backing with your tool to make

Density of shag

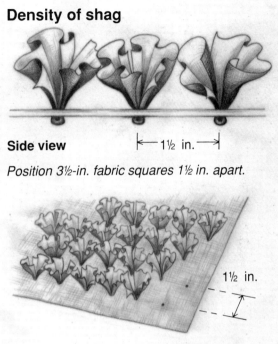

Side view |← 1½ in. →|

Position 3½-in. fabric squares 1½ in. apart.

1½ in.

Stagger rows of 3½-in. squares 1½ in. apart.

Successful fabric shag comes from equally spacing squares or circles to avoid thick and thin areas.

an opening. With a fabric square in one hand, place the point of the tool in the center of the cloth square or circle. Fold the fabric over the point of the tool and poke both fabric and tool through the hole made in the backing. Force the material in just enough to hold it, about ¼ in. to ⅜ in.

As you're poking the fabric squares through the backing to create the shag, keep even spacing in mind. You might think just placing these squares at random would work, but it doesn't. It's far better to space them evenly so you don't get thin and thick areas. The density for an average shag pile using 3½-in. fabric squares is one square of fabric for every 1½ in. of backing canvas. Squares placed too closely together may look squeezed, while those positioned too far apart will cause the fabric to flop and look sparse.

If there's any possibility of the backing showing through the shag, I hook a low background, both for the sake of appearance and wearability. In the

Highly reflective Mylar can be dramatic when cut in ⅛-in. strips and hooked (here amid rows of cotton crochet yarn) or worked as shag.

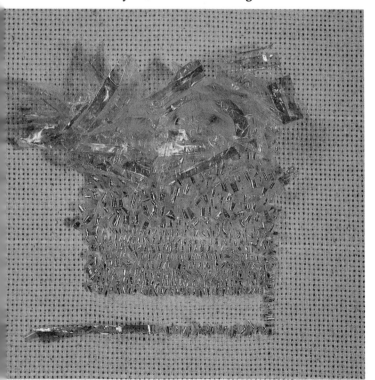

Iridescent plasticized gift wrap produces wonderful effects, whether cut in ½-in. strips and hooked in short and medium loops (at bottom of sample) or worked as shag.

case of rugs and pillows that will get a lot of use, I always hook a good foundation for fabric shag, which also equalizes the tension on the backing with that in the rest of the hooked areas. Sometimes I seize this opportunity to use surplus fabric or yarn for the background, since very little shows. I always keep the colors compatible with the shag, however.

When making fabric and color selections for shag, be reassured that it's difficult to make poor selections for this technique. A wild mixture will be glorious fun, yet all one color and fabric will be just as suitable. I'm always surprised, however, how many different colors and patterns it takes to make a successful mixture, usually about 20. It seems that the offbeat materials mix in with the common ones, the thick with the thin, the print with the plain—and, of course, I thrive on the unusual thrown in too.

With a mixed combination, color selections are made just as they are with yarns. All printed, plain and textured fabrics are piled on the floor. The materials that don't work are easily spotted and thrown out. It's surprising how much material is needed for shag, so always add far more than you would expect. For example, an average square foot of backing canvas will take about 150 to 175 fabric squares cut to 3¼ in. and set fairly close. A normal mix for that number of squares may contain up to 40 or more different fabrics.

As if these combinations weren't enough, I often like to juxtapose these fabrics with metallics, metal springs, paper, plastic or some other surprise. I enjoy what the unexpected does to the already beautiful contrasts. Wall hangings give you the freedom to add any of these unusual materials, but with floor rugs, you must be more selective.

Once the shag surface is completed, each square must be secured well on the backing. If the piece will be on public display, you can count on viewers pulling these squares when no one is looking. People can't resist tugging at them to see how well they're anchored and how you made them.

To secure the shag, turn the piece to the wrong side, where you will see a series of uniform "noses"—the tips of the shag protruding through the backing. Using a flexible adhesive (Tacky Glue or Super Tacky), circle each nose with glue to bond the fabric and backing together. When dry,

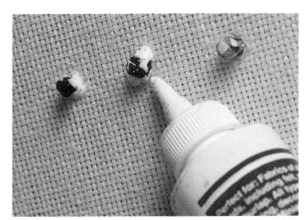

Fabric shag is bonded to the backing canvas by running a bead of flexible adhesive around each nose that protrudes on the wrong side of the canvas. For clarity's sake, only three noses are shown in this photo, but in reality many more would likely be clustered together.

Low shag is created by using small fabric squares and cutting the edges of the completed shag close to the surface.

this bond will be strong enough to hold until the entire surface is covered with latex in the final finishing stages (see pp. 112-113).

The process of creating low shag varies only slightly from that used to work high shag. Cut the fabric in 1-in. to 1½-in. squares, preferably on the bias, then poke them into the backing very close together. After all the squares are permanently secured, cut the surface even with a large pair of scissors to whatever depth of pile you desire. Low shag can be worked in any fabric and usually holds up well due to the density of the surface pile.

Another variation on shag is what I call reverse shag. I realized that each time I turned a shag section to the wrong side, I was as thrilled with the noses on the back as I was with the shag on the front. So I decided to put the noses to use as a new surface texture. Reverse shag is shown in the photo at right.

To work reverse shag, cut the fabric squares to minimum size and poke them through the backing very close together, working from the wrong side. After poking, clip the excess fabric to ¼ in. from the surface. Immediately secure the new noses on the wrong side with flexible adhesive to keep them from popping out. When completed, reverse shag produces little points of fabric that jut out from the backing, with an entirely different effect from regular shag.

Reverse shag is created by pushing very small squares of fabric through the canvas from the back side, so the noses poke through the front. Here, the multicolored noses decorating the low hooked background are whimsically reminiscent of fabric beads or buttons.

Sculpted, dimensional shapes can be created by densely hooking with the punch needle. First create the outline with the shortest loop length, hooking the loops as close together as possible.

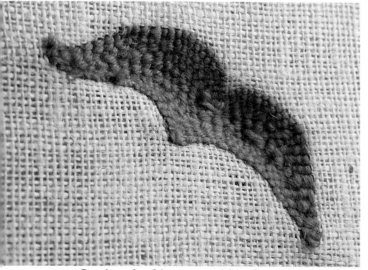

Continue hooking rows within the outline, working toward the center and lengthening the loops with every new row. Pack the rows in very tightly and stitch over existing center rows several times to ensure a dense pile. The canvas will take on a concave bulge as the hooking reaches completion.

Sculpted technique

Of all the hooking techniques, sculpting—which produces carved, dimensional shapes—is my favorite. The moment the tightly packed yarns are cut, they change magically into brilliant tones and rich, velvety textures. Unfortunately, this is also the slowest and most tedious of all the hooking techniques I use. But I can't resist it, and the effects are well worth it.

The shapes are created by first varying the loop lengths, using a short loop for background and longer loops for the areas being sculpted. The variety of loop lengths used for the sculpted areas depends on the design and the contour you want to produce. (If you wanted to work a dome shape, for example, you would gradually increase the loop length from the outside of the circle to the center of the dome. If you wanted the surface to undulate, you would work a series of gradually longer and shorter loops according to your design.) Once the areas to be sculpted are densely hooked, the loops of yarn are cut to produce a smooth surface—something like giving the yarn a haircut. You can use either the punch needle or the speed needle for sculpted work, but when you're learning the technique, the punch needle offers greater control.

I prefer to use inexpensive, synthetic four-ply knitting worsteds for sculpting, because the yarns need not be of exquisite quality to produce good results when they are packed close together. The softness and sheen of synthetics also creates a richness that's often lacking in wool. If I'm matching background or repeating colors or texture, however, I will use wool.

For a first attempt at sculpting, start with a small shape, for example, a 1-in. circle or leaf form. To begin, set the punch needle on the shortest loop (No. 12) and hook the outline of the shape, working in a circle and keeping the loops as close together as possible. Do this by placing a stitch in every hole of the outline. For the second row, change the punch needle to the next longest loop (No. 11) and hook close to the original outside row, packing the loops close together. For the third row, change again to the next longest loop (No. 10) and continue as before. At the fourth row, change to No. 9 to create the crown of the form. Without changing the loops any more, continue

filling in rows toward the center, packing them in tightly until all the backing is filled in.

When you think you've finished hooking, take another look at the right side of the canvas. Press down on the hooked loops with your fingers and try to visualize the pressure the sculpted form will eventually take, whether from being walked on if it's a rug or sat upon if it's used as upholstery. What you want to see is dense hooking in the area being sculpted, which will prevent this area from being flattened out with use. I usually find that I need to hook several more rows in the center to make a good, firm shape. The difference between good and poor quality is often just two or three rows of hooking. So, even though you can't see any more backing canvas, add a few more rows of stitching in the center, going over already hooked areas to increase their density.

From the right side, the uncut shapes will look awkward, messy and uneven, and some of the loops may have been accidentally split by hooking so densely. You'll also notice that the loops in the very center of the form seem longer, even though you haven't change the needle to another setting. All of this is perfectly normal and is caused by the tension of the tightly packed yarns compressing the loops and pushing the backing fabric into a convex shape.

You are now ready to start trimming your sculpted form. Beginning at the outside edge, use a large scissors to cut away all uneven surface loops. At this stage, you're cutting only the high, excess loops to get a preliminary form established. Keep the scissor blades flat and horizontal to the surface, and make sure not to clip the backing material, which is a very easy mistake to make. You

From the right side, the loops will look uneven and messy (top photo). Press the hooked area with your fingers to see if you meet firm resistance. If so, the area is hooked densely enough and is ready to trim.

The trimming begins with large scissors (middle photo) to cut away excess yarn and establish the preliminary sculpted form.

Final trimming is done with small, sharp-pointed embroidery shears (bottom photo). Clip all uncut loops and refine the shape, taking care not to cut into the backing material accidentally.

These details from *Metro-Plex* (seen in full on p. 89) demonstrate the visual impact and textural dimension that sculpted forms can bring to a hooked piece.

should produce a fairly smooth, even shape, although some uncut loops will still be buried beneath the tightly hooked surface. Using small embroidery scissors, cut all these loops open. A beautiful, smooth shape will begin to emerge.

By now, the surface will have excess fuzz, which should be removed as you continue cutting. Removing this fuzz will let you see where you are cutting and will prevent the debris from working itself permanently into the rest of the piece. You can remove most of the fuzz by tipping the frame face down and giving it a few gentle pats from the back. A piece of plastic laid on the floor to collect all these clippings is helpful. (I often save these fuzzy remnants for felting or spinning, especially if they are a luscious color.) To clean the remaining fuzz from the surface, I use a hand-held vacuum nozzle, using air suction only, never any brushes.

I've learned to keep a tank-type vacuum at my side during all this clipping.

When sculpting with the speed hook, I follow the same procedure, starting with hooking the outside row on the shortest loop. Then, according to my design and the effect I want to produce, I adjust the setscrew to vary the loop length for the pile height needed in the sculpted area. As always, you'll probably need to add a couple of rows more than you expected to the center area to make it dense and firm. Once you get used to turning the speed hook in all directions, using it for this technique is as easy as using the punch needle. Just remember to leave the point of the speed needle firmly in the backing while turning to a different direction. Otherwise, you will pull out the stitches just worked.

Because sculpting is a slow and tiring process, I hook one shape at a time and clip it immediately. One bad case of blisters taught me never to do all the cutting for a sculpted piece at once. I now protect my scissor fingers by putting masking tape around the thumb and ring finger where the scissors rub. Bandaids don't work as well, since they often slip off from the friction and leave a sticky residue on your finger. Be sure to tape your fingers before you start to cut, not after your fingers are already sore.

A good example of overenthusiasm for this sculpted technique is an antique rocker that I completed 25 years ago (see the photo on p. 100). I was so thrilled to have acquired my first antique as well as to be using this new hooking technique that I designed sculpted upholstery especially for the rocker. I spent over three weeks, working more than 40 hours a week, to complete it, and my fingers took a real beating in the process. Over the years, of course, my fingers have healed. But I learned never to do an all-sculpted area this large. Now I combine this beautiful technique with others, using it as an accent. On the plus side, the chair has held up well to a lot of wear and tear. For many years the rocker was used daily in front of the TV by two children and occasional dogs. It was washed once (by hand) and still looks good. The brilliant color has faded from the sun to a subtle softness, but the high carved shapes have never flattened out even the slightest. And, if I ever found the time or patience (or courage), I could

clip it all again to remove the thin faded layer of yarn on the surface and have the vivid jewel tones back again, just as they were the day I finished it.

Reverse hooking

I so enjoy the flat look of the raw, unhooked backing before it's totally filled in that I often achieve a similar feel by reversing my hooking—that is to say, I hook on the right side of the canvas. After the main areas and sculpting are completed, I turn the work over and fill in the exposed backing, hooking this time from the finished (front) side of the work. This technique cre-

In reverse hooking, short loops are worked from the right rather than wrong side of the canvas and produce very flat stitches. Here, white synthetic cord has been reverse-hooked between bands of regularly hooked rug wool.

Several techniques were used in one section of the wall piece *Quadro-Plex*, all worked while the piece was still in the frame, taut and easy to control. First, acrylic paint was applied to the inside of each grid square to provide background color where no hooking was to be done.

ates a very flat surface, which looks just like the back of most work. It's used whenever the backing must be covered, when wearability is an issue and when a painted or exposed backing is undesirable — all common factors in floor rugs.

More often than not, I use a contrasting yarn for the reverse hooking, which outlines and enhances the adjacent higher piles. For example, when the sculpted shape is in wool, I may use a shiny rayon yarn in a different color both to accentuate the dimension of the sculpted shape and to highlight the main design. Whenever I think that background loops will destroy the effect of the sculpted work

or obliterate an intended clean shape in a design, I use reversed hooking.

Reversed hooking often requires more precision than regular hooking. The reason for this is that you're working in and around the longer loops already finished, which challenges your ability to make even stitches. For this reason, it's best to use the punch needle set for the shortest loop. The loops that protrude on the back of the work will be latexed just like the surrounding flat areas during the finishing stage (see Chapter 4). Once the reversed hooking is finished, it will wear and perform just like regular hooking.

Next, metal washers, spray-painted bronze, were glued down, then protected with plastic vials the same diameter as the washers. The assembly was weighted with heavy books overnight to ensure a good bond.

Caulking was applied from the back of the canvas with a caulking gun and a metal knife. It was squirted into the center of each washer and, with the frame propped up to prevent crushing the hooking, allowed to seep through to the right side.

Dyes, paint and other decorative finishes

There are many other ways of getting the right color or texture into a piece besides hooking. Dyes and paints applied to the backing material can provide an evenly colored background for a work, or they can liven up dull yarns or yardage. Even unusual materials like caulking compounds can lend a new surface texture.

I've never enjoyed dyeing anything. It makes me impatient, and I resent the time this additional process takes away from my work. But because practical answers often win out, I've discovered over the years that dyes can give certain results to yarns and materials for hooking that can't be obtained any other way.

I dye, or over-dye, to use up excess yarns, to combine leftovers or to get a color quickly that would take much longer to get by mail order or a shopping trip. I use the most readily available dye, Rit, from the local grocery store. I dye small quantities of fabric and yarns in a pot on the stove, stirring often and removing them when the color looks right. For variegated effects, I just don't stir as often, which pleases me.

I've had the best success with dyeing in the washing machine, but this should be used only for

Finished view (above) of the four-part wall work *Quadro-Plex* (1989, 120 in. by 120 in. by 6 in.) and a detail (below) showing the texture of the caulking after it was painted with metallic paint. (Photo above by Roger Schreiber, Seattle.)

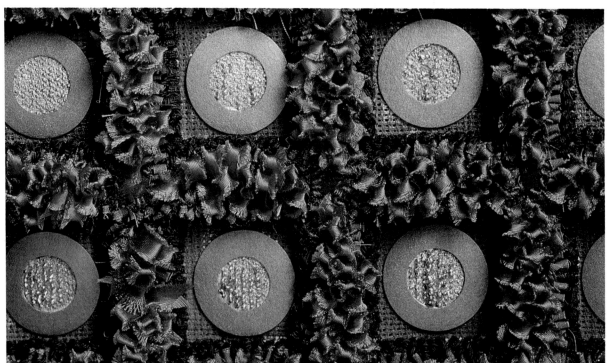

large quantities because it's not easy to duplicate colors from load to load. I carry boiling water to the machine to fill it, add the Rit by the package, mix it well and then add the wet yarn. I watch the color of the fiber as it dyes and turn the machine on occasionally to ensure even distribution of the dye. But I'm careful not to leave it on too long, since excess agitation would shrink the wools. When I've gotten the color I want, I drain the machine and add the same temperature water to rinse the fiber well. The water must run clear to prevent further bleeding of the dye. I'm careful not to wring the skeins, but squeeze them gently in toweling, shake them a bit and then hang them outdoors to drip dry.

As you can tell, my approach is to use the quickest and simplest methods, with the least math and the shortest amount of time involved. My apologies go out to professional dyers, who are masters of their craft, for endorsing such a crude approach. I truly admire their patience and the beautiful results they achieve. My nonprofessional method may work for you, but if you are interested in creating high-quality dyed textiles, I recommend that you scout out the many good books written on the subject. There are also numerous dyeing workshops held around the country, which may be of interest to you. Learning the techniques of dyeing is an art in itself, one that may lead you to all sorts of new explorations in fiber.

For me, paint is a fabric dye. It's a quick and easy way to control and change color. Covering an unhooked background with paint is a technique I use frequently when I want the backing material to show but be another color. Paint is also a must when creating sculpted forms, because it further enhances the relief of the dimensional form. I use water-soluble paint in tubes, which come in a good range of colors and can easily be thinned to an appropriate consistency. As mentioned earlier, if the paint adds an unwanted stiffness to your work, use a fabric paint like Versatex.

Canned spray paint from the paint store is another color option. It's so fast and easy that I use it whenever possible. One drawback is that it's difficult to control and can't be used effectively where you want a very specific amount of color. I reserve it for special cases, like a light overall spray to shade a work or for random color on a shag. Some of my favorite spray-paint colors are the metallics —silver, gold and copper. Applied to the back of yardage, spray paint adds a stiffness I like—you can't tell if the material is cloth or paper. This approach is good on shags to produce a two-toned effect and make both sides of the fabric squares attractive. I often use spray paints on metals, painting them with a metallic finish to enhance their look.

A word of caution: Spray paint is toxic, and the fumes can cause headaches and other problems. Use it only in well-ventilated areas, and always wear a mask. It's best to spray outdoors, but if you must work indoors, be sure to open the windows.

Another unusual material I use for a decorative finish is caulking compound. By now, you probably realize that I'll try anything to achieve an interesting effect, texture or bonding in my work. Caulking compound will do all three. I don't use this material often, but if I want to cover the backing weave completely, add a change of texture and color or, most important, apply an adhesive that will do both, this is my choice. The adhesive type of compound will bond metals, plastics and heavy objects to fiber when other adhesives fail.

Caulking compound can be found in any hardware store. It is available in many types and colors, ranging from black, brown and beige to white and transparent. The compound is applied using a caulking gun, a basic tool used in the building trades. If more control is needed than is possible with the gun, you can spread the caulking with a knife. You can produce both highly textured and very smooth surfaces with caulking since it's very thick and manageable.

Caulking compound generally takes several hours to dry, which gives you ample time to add elements to the surface. Unusual textures and color are possible by adding bits of fabric, metal shavings, sawdust, yarn clippings (perhaps from sculpting), dry pigments and other materials. And when the surface is dry, it can be painted.

At this time, I use caulking compounds mainly on wall hangings. I don't recommend it for floor rugs or in any large areas of a piece, because it's stiff, though flexible. Also, it hasn't been tested over a long time for fiber breakage, so I don't know how it would hold up. But if you're looking for a backing cover, unique texture and adhesive all in one, caulking compound is a modern answer.

Curls, bows, ties and additions

Curls, bows and other additions incorporated into a hooked piece can add a new dimension to your work. So few fiber workers seem to take advantage of the potential of these fabric additions. They can add a little pizzazz to a piece, differentiate a high texture from a shag or simply be used as a decorative method of securing other objects.

Creating fabric and ribbon curls to include in hooked pieces is a technique I devised to add a whimsical quality to the work. I like adding humor to my pieces, and these curls seem to make anybody who sees them smile. The discovery of this technique is a good illustration of the way one idea can lead to another. Curls were a result of my work with metal springs and research with adhesives. They may look difficult to make, but they're really quite simple.

Use any type of fabric strip, cut ¼ in. wide on the bias or straight grain. You can also use ribbon, cord or yarn. A nonporous dowel is needed as a form on which to make the curls. This dowel can be a plastic soda straw, a metal knitting needle, tubing or a glass rod.

Cut the fabric strip approximately 30 in. long —a length that will completely wrap a plastic straw. Dip the fabric strip into a diluted glue solution made from ten parts water to one part white glue. Lift the strip out and remove the excess glue by pulling the strip through your extended index and middle fingers (see the top photo at left). Wrap the saturated strip around the dowel as if you were making a spring, gently pushing the edges together. The wet fabric sticks to the dowel, making it easy to control. If the ends unwind and won't stick, secure them with a hair clip or pin, preferably one that won't rust.

A variation of this process is used for fabrics with dense naps, like velour or velvet, and for shiny materials like metallics or satins, whose surface textures would be lost if saturated with glue. Do not dip strips of these fabrics into the adhesive. Instead, cover the dowel with undiluted white glue, spread evenly. Then wrap the fabric around the dowel, to which it should adhere.

With either method, let the curl dry, then remove the dowel carefully. Don't unwind the strip from the dowel. Instead, pinch the plastic straw or twist the rod to loosen the curl. Slide the fabric

Fabric curls are made by dipping cloth strips or lengths of ribbon into a diluted glue solution, as shown at top. The excess glue is squeezed off in preparation for wrapping the saturated ribbon around a nonporous dowel.

The wet strip is wrapped around a dowel (in the photo above, a plastic soda straw) with the edges of the strip pushed together. Hair clips secure the ribbon ends to the straw. Dried overnight, the curls are removed by twisting the rod and sliding them off.

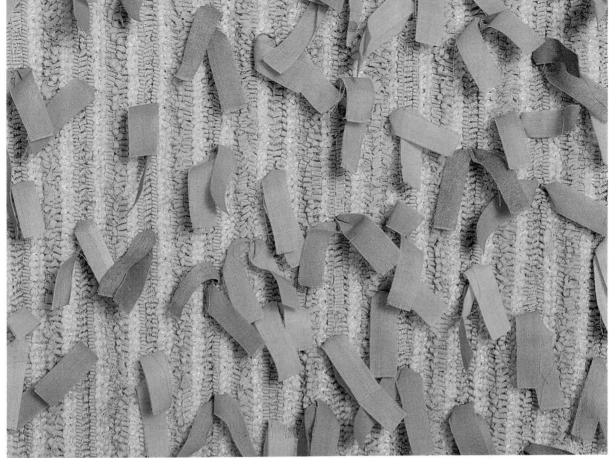

This detail of *Glad Raggs* shows ½-in. strips integrated into a low hooked background. The strips were poked with a chopstick from the front to the back of the canvas and then out the front again. They were later secured by the latex applied to the entire back of the work to seal it.

strip off the dowel, and check to see if it retains its curl. If it doesn't, add more adhesive to the solution. If it seems too stiff, dilute the solution more.

This technique automatically brings to mind many other novel treatments. One interesting approach I have found is to wrap any metal rod or knitting needle with a ¼-in. synthetic strip, using no glue. Secure the ends with clips and place the wrapped rod in your oven on clean oven racks or a cookie sheet for 20 minutes at approximately 250°F. This heat-set process will give your synthetic strips a permanent curl without adhesives. Each synthetic fabric will set differently, so try experimenting with a variety of fabrics and textures. The results can be sensational.

The idea of using fabric bows and ties came from a multistriped remnant someone gave me. The colors were soft pastels, exactly those I was using in my multicolored work titled *Glad Raggs*.

I'd already used a high cotton shag for one section but needed a similar dimension for another section. My original intention was to cut each strip separately and hook them in a long loop. Seeing those multicolored ribbons waving about made me realize that they would be lost if I hooked them into ordinary loops, so I started finding different ways of tying the ½-in. strips onto the work. Making an opening by using my chopstick as a poking tool, I used a large crochet hook to push one end through to the back and then pulled it up to the surface again. With lightweight cottons, this simple poking technique would be enough to secure the tie until it's sealed with latex later. For a stronger hold, I would secure them with either a single tie or a square knot.

Although the striped strips were cut on the straight grain, there was little cause for concern about raveling. The ribbons were tied or secured

These multicolored, tied additions in *Razzle-Dazzle* were cut from striped fabric, giving two colors to each 1-in. cloth strip. When folded and pressed, they made vivid two-toned ties.

well, which prevented the threads from ever coming off. Any separation or raveling only added to the soft, thready look of the overall texture.

I was so pleased with this new texture that I ran out shopping and found three different color selections to add to other works. One stripe was promptly used in *Razzle-Dazzle,* an art rug whose vivid explosion of color called for a heavier mass of bows or ties. I cut 1-in. ribbons from the striped fabric and then folded and pressed them so they formed a two-toned tie with a different color on each side. Such uses of striped fabrics and their double effects can cause your mind to reel with possibilities. Any cut yardage, in any length or width, will give the same or similar effects. By experimenting with ribbons, cords and other cut fabrics, you can achieve some novel textures and patterns—all tied on instead of hooked.

If you can't get the effect you want with any of the other techniques, adding beads or embroidery can often be just the embellishment the work needs. I view the metal washers I use on large projects as no more than sequins on a grand scale. I've used beads and embroidery to a limited extent in my hooked projects, and their potential on hooked wearables intrigues me.

As you can see from the examples in this chapter, the range of materials available today for hooking is virtually endless. Each brings a new color, texture or dimension to a piece and will spur you on to try even more. A fabric that seems boring often comes to life when cut in strips, or when hooked in combination with a shiny plastic or an unusual metallic. Once you start these hooked variations, you'll never look at fabric and fiber — or any material — the same way again.

Working positions

Everyone has a favorite working position for making hooked projects. You must find what suits you best and consider all ways to make your work as enjoyable as possible. Good light and comfortable posture encourage longer hooking hours as well as more productive and rewarding sessions.

With a small lap frame, a sitting position is a natural working position. You can sit anywhere there's a table or other object on which to prop the frame. You shouldn't have any back problems when working on this frame, because you can just turn it around to reach the area you're working on more easily.

If you are hooking on a large upright frame, you'll need a different working position. The ideal arrangement is to be able to hook on the wrong side of the work, yet still be able to walk around to see the right side without moving the frame. I accomplish this by leaning the frame against a ceiling beam or in the window well of my angled ceiling. The frame is usually not tall enough to reach the beam, so I place it on a coffee table, my weaving bench or anything that raises it and supports it firmly. If there's no convenient prop, create additional height on the frame by securing two 2-in. by 2-in. pieces of wood with C-clamps to the top of the frame. With these wood extensions in place, the frame can rest securely within a window well or against a ceiling beam.

Upright frames of any size can be leaned against any wall, window or other stable structure. For shorter frames, rest them on a table or bench that puts them at a height at which you can work comfortably. If the frame leans against the wall, you'll have to move it away from the wall to view the finished work, but usually this is not a real inconvenience. The important thing to remember when propping upright frames is that the bottom of the frame must be braced to prevent it from sliding. Placing a heavy object on

Working on the lap frame in a sitting position is easy and comfortable, because you can rest the frame on the edge of any surface and quickly turn it to reach any part of the canvas.

Large canvases are best worked from a standing position. Here the frame is supported on a small bench and braced in the window well. Bricks at the bottom of the frame prevent it from moving during hooking.

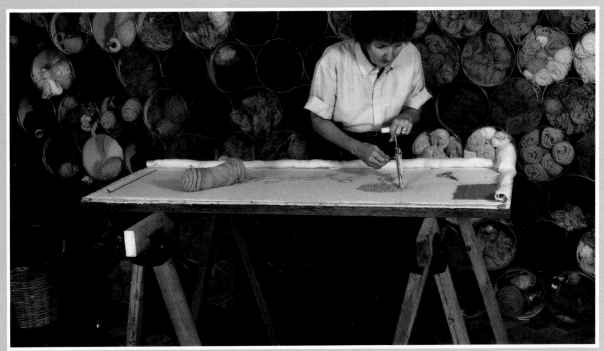

Many people work with the frame positioned horizontally, but bending over the work can quickly prove uncomfortable. To work horizontally, prop the frame on any two supports of equal height that won't interfere with the hooking needle's progress.

each side of the frame at its base usually eliminates any problems. I use anything handy as a weight, like my 20-lb. tailor's iron on one side and a 25-lb. iron vise on the other. A couple of bricks or cement blocks also work well. If they're dirty, put them in plastic bags to avoid soiling any yarns or fabrics.

To avoid aching muscles and a sore back, I move around frequently — which working upright allows. In fact, I spend a lot of time walking around to the other side of the work to study it, which helps keep me limber. Some people use a mirror to see the other side, but I prefer seeing the whole of the image so I can make better color and design decisions. Sometimes when I'm working on the lower areas of a canvas, I'll sit on the floor, then move to a 10-in. stool. I have stools of several heights so that as I work on different areas of a piece, I switch seats and always stay comfortable.

Don't forget standing as an option for hooking — half my time is spent this way. When using the speed needle, you'll be able to maintain better pressure on the backing as well as go much faster when you're standing. And it's good for the posture.

Hooking with the work in a horizontal position is probably the most common approach, but my back hurts just looking at this setup. If you want to work horizontally, you can do so easily with any frame. Just rest both ends on a pair of tables, stools or saw horses of the same height. You can also simply place the frame flat on a tabletop, but the frame may need to be elevated a few inches to prevent the hook or needle from hitting the table. There are a few special effects I occasionally work that require using the frame in this position, but, for the most part, it's my least favorite position, because it becomes very uncomfortable after hooking for just a short time.

3

Color and Design

When faced with an empty canvas waiting to be hooked, you may react like a schoolchild who is given a blank piece of paper and told to write. The mind goes numb and fear sets in. What should I make? Will it look good? What if I don't like it? These are questions that novice and experienced hooking enthusiasts alike often ask themselves. But once you realize that there are no set rules to follow and that mistakes can be ripped out more easily than they went in, a sense of freedom and confidence develops.

I laugh when people ask me where I get all my ideas. It takes only three or four projects to keep

Detail of Quadro-Plex, a four-part wall work. The full piece is shown on p. 72.

me busy for an entire year. Finding inspiration and keeping an active imagination do take work, but what enjoyable work it is! Going to galleries, museums and art shows, keeping up on art, interior design and fashion—all these activities are the "work" required to find fresh ideas. It's visual research, not much different from investigation done in other fields—except you're learning to "see," not merely to look. This means focusing your concentration and thinking differently about objects usually taken for granted. Shapes, colors, textures and images now take on a different light when seen in relationship to design possibilities.

In making this effort to see, try to study the best, be it in art, fashion, architecture, decorating or fiber work. Just as important as staying in touch with contemporary art and design developments is learning to look inside yourself and discover what you truly enjoy. Force yourself to look in depth at things, and ask yourself—and really try to answer—such questions as, "Why do or don't I like this?" and "What was the maker trying to say?" Just as good cooks study recipes both old and new, always testing and improvising to suit their individual tastes, so, too, will you learn to refine your ideas and style in your fiber projects. Answering questions like those posed above will help you develop your own tastes and individuality.

Ideas don't always come from what you see but from what you think you see. This happens to me often. I catch a glimpse of something out of the corner of my eye, then it's gone. I really don't know what it was, but I do know it was worth remembering. From experience, I've found it best not to investigate these blurred images any further. The disappointment of seeing the actual thing often destroys the wonder of the imagined. Usually I try to recreate the essence of what I glimpsed, using it as inspiration for fiber expression.

When you get a wild idea, it takes a lot of nerve to design and execute it. Keep in mind that there is no supreme "fiber judge," and that there are no rules that can't be broken. Fiber purists may shudder at the unusual materials and techniques I use in my hooked pieces, but it's the diversity that keeps me totally involved. The goal is to create something you're proud of, something that expresses your individual style. I hope you will gain as much satisfaction in the process as I do.

Designing with color, texture and technique

With the highly tactile surfaces that rug-hooking tools allow and the many materials that can be used, it's often difficult to separate design from color, texture or technique. Individual projects may be dominated by one element or another, but most remain so interrelated that they blend as one. Wall hangings have different requirements from floor rugs; wearables have different needs still. Each project should be designed to meet its specific set of requirements.

Some people approach their blank canvas by using basic principles of design, such as visual balance, repetition, scale or harmony. Others may be influenced by paintings, graphic elements or a favorite range of colors. Inspiration can come from the geometry of buildings or the organic shapes of nature. I'm always aware and "seeing," seeking inspiration from things as diverse as museums and fashion to magazines on architecture and design. Another possible source of inspiration might be the design section of your local library or a bookstore with a good selection of art and design books. Explore what seems most suitable to you and your intentions.

Sometimes the most unusual decisions can dictate a design. Such was the case with an early floor rug of mine called *Fiesta*, worked in 1973. My original goal in making this rug was to use up the many small remnants of cotton I had left over from my sewing days. As such, the design was controlled by the limitations of the material on hand. It had to be made up of small quantities of color-compatible fabrics, yet designed with some repetition to control so much visual activity. Wearability, washability, color compatibility and available materials were given equal consideration in the eventual design.

Because my supply of scraps was so large, the rug was designed to be a generous 5 ft. 7 in. by 8½ ft. I sorted the wild collection of remnants, piling related colors together in groups, discarding pastels and allowing only cotton or cotton blends. To plan color, I divided each pile in half so there would be an equal balance of color at each end of the rug. I in-

Detail of *Fiesta* (1973, 102 in. by 67 in.). This piece was hooked with ¼-in. pile from multicolor cotton strips in two large sections, which were later seamed. (Photo by the author.)

In *Square Roots* (1987, 48½ in. by 57 in.), the author painted the linen backing material to create a texture that contrasts with the hooked fibers. (Collection of Dr. and Mrs. John Thurlow, Lacey, Washington; photo by Roger Schreiber, Seattle.)

East/West (1987, 48 in. by 78 in.) has a monochromatic color scheme. The piece's simple design and subtle color range play off its textures and sculpted forms. (Photo by Roger Schreiber, Seattle.)

tentionally designed large circle shapes to use the multitudes of very small scraps in broken, but balanced, colors. The horizontal rows were reserved for materials in larger quantities, which also gave a bit more organization to the broken color in the circles. The difficulty was finding a suitable quantity of darker colors to balance the wider borders needed on each end.

I realized that a large quantity of fabric strips would be needed, so it was easy to decide on pile height. I wanted a flat, ¼-in. pile (No. 10 setting on the punch needle), with the loops worked close together for durability since the piece would be used as a floor rug. I knew that cotton wears well if it's hooked densely, but it soils easily. With this in mind, I decided to make the rug in two pieces and join it in the center with machine stitching. This gave me the option of later separating the pieces in order to wash them more easily.

Calculating the amount of material needed was critical with this design. I didn't dare use a color or print unless there was enough to extend across the entire width of the rug in more than just a couple of rows. Until this time, I had only "guesstimated" on quantities of materials needed in my work. With *Fiesta*, I learned to figure exact quantities ahead of time. I worked out a very easy method that I still use to this day (see the sidebar on pp. 91-92), but I wasn't at all prepared for the tremendous amount or material required. It became immediately obvious that my supply was drastically short, and I ended up begging friends to sew and quickly learning where the best buys on yardage were to be found. The final piece used over 80 sq. yd. of material.

Ever the optimist, I estimated that the rug would take about three or four months to complete. Six months later, it was finished. (This was before I discovered adhesives or the speed hook or had much experience. Today it would probably take me about three-and-one-half months.) When *Fiesta* was placed in exhibitions and was graciously accepted for a traveling show, I felt it was all truly worth it.

This elation came to a sudden halt three months later, however, when I learned that the rug had been stolen. I couldn't believe that anything this large and heavy would be taken. Optimistic as ever, I had a feeling inside that I would get it back.

Four months later it was recovered by the police, so filthy it looked as if it had been in the middle of a highway. The dirt on the piece hid its colors, but fortunately there were no signs of wear.

Because I had originally made the rug in two sections for easier laundering, I took it apart and soaked each half in the bathtub with warm water and detergent. Five separate sudsings and rinsings later, the water was clear. Each section was then hung over sturdy wooden rods and allowed to drip dry. I was careful not to wring or twist it, to avoid further crushing or wrinkling of the nap. The rug was allowed to dry undisturbed—it took more than ten days—except for an occasional shaking to fluff it. When the two sections were sewn back together by machine, the rug looked as good as new. In fact, the piece has been exhibited many times since the incident, and no one has been any the wiser—until now.

Color

Working with color in fiber differs greatly from working with color in other media. Fiber has dimension and texture, and it picks up shadows and reflects light and color very differently from other flat media. For these reasons, I rely solely on my eye and instincts when selecting yarns and yardage. In spite of all the color charts and theories available, I trust my own judgment in seeing how fibers and color affect one another, and in seeing what happens when rough texture is juxtaposed with smooth, or shiny with dull. When working with strong textures, color never remains constant or predictable, and it can appear very different in different settings. Developing your own color sense takes some study, time and effort; and along the way you must keep asking yourself which colors appeal to you, which don't and why. With a little experience, your own inner judgment will develop.

To make decisions about color, texture and materials, I still find the throw-it-on-the-floor approach (as described on p. 46) the most reliable one for me. With this approach I can quickly see what fits or what must be discarded. The materials speak for themselves.

Some of the most attractive work with color is done with monotones, that is, with colors all in the same family. This approach to designing is one of my favorites, because it allows a great amount of freedom to use combinations of textures, materials and techniques without the concern of clashing colors. Working in this way also trains your eye really to see color. For example, in my all-white works like *Creme-de-la-Creme* (shown on the cover), it may seem that the materials are all one color. But look closely, and you'll discover a wide variety o.f tones.

As an exercise in seeing, try piling together every white yarn and fabric that you have. You'll find that some look yellow, others blue, some just plain dirty. The same is true with black and other monotones. But even the colors that look unappealing on their own can be quite lovely when mixed in the right combination in a work. I've learned that there is no such thing as an ugly color; if a color looks ugly, it's because it has been used in the wrong way.

The irregular shape and vivid colors of *Metro-II* (1988, 57 in. by 84 in.) enliven the floor of a dressing room. (Collection of Mr. and Mrs. Edward Elson, New York City.)

Designing rugs

I have many passions, but without a doubt, rugs are at the top of my list. If producing rugs were more economically feasible, I would do nothing else. But one house can hold only so many rugs, and I don't feel that I can give them away. So I exhibit and sell a rug every chance I get.

My rugs began as area rugs for the floor, but with the addition of nontraditional materials, they are now better labeled "art rugs." This term seems a bit more descriptive and implies that the works can go anywhere—on walls or floors, in private interiors or public spaces. Along with other changes, like the addition of nonfiber elements, my art rugs have evolved from conventional, rectangular shapes into irregular polygons and asymmetrical forms. These irregular variations continue to intrigue me. I enjoy the way the works can be adjusted to suit different interiors. They offer greater variety for furniture arrangements and are very versatile when used as wall pieces.

Although many of my rugs end up on the wall, most are made for the floor. I enjoy the discipline required to design for the floor. The word "rug" implies high-quality workmanship. One expects that a rug should wear well, take abuse and look good for years.

A rug is the easiest of all projects to design. When you consider the many limiting factors, there are really few decisions left to be made. To a great extent, location, size, color, material, technique and mood all dictate what the final design will be. Once you've worked out the needs of all these factors, your design is fairly well along.

When designing a project, I like to have a defined space in which the work will end up. If I don't have a real one, I imagine one. I much prefer this approach to making a rug and then trying to find a spot for it later. The location automatically sets the design direction. For example, you'd naturally design a rug differently for a family with small children than for wealthy socialites.

Ambience is as important as all the other design factors. I like to get a feeling for the room as a whole and for any other space that the rug will affect. I decide what role the rug will play and what mood I want it to project. It may be the center of

Knowing that the corner of a floor rug would take a lot of wear from foot traffic, the author incorporated an irregular corner into the design of *Pieces of Nine* (1987, 58 in. by 78 in.), a rug hooked in wool with silver metallic highlights.

interest or a subdued accent. It may be refined and sophisticated or humorous and playful. This design element is an important consideration, since unless it's planned otherwise, a highly textured or colorful rug — as most hooked rugs are — can easily dominate a room.

To get a sense of the rug's basic size and shape, I start by playing with unprinted newsprint or any plain paper. (For rugs larger than the paper, tape pieces together.) Fold the edges under — there's no need to cut — until you have the size you want. Place the paper on the floor in the rug's final location and visualize different shapes and sizes. The rug doesn't have to be rectangular — think round or irregular. The paper allows quick experimentation without cost or loss. When I'm stumped and feel I haven't an idea in the world, I just lay out this paper, and my mind flies in a million directions, imagining the wildest shapes.

Pieces of Nine and *Corporate Sails* were both designed in this way. When I saw the paper shapes for *Pieces of Nine* in place, it became immediately obvious that the heavily trafficked corner would take a beating. Why not take the corner off? By using the grid and a stepped design, I satisfied my love for irregular and unusual shapes

Corporate Sails (1986, 90 in. by 46 in.), originally designed as a rug, now hangs in a stairwell. (Collection of Mr. and Mrs. Edward Elson, New York City.)

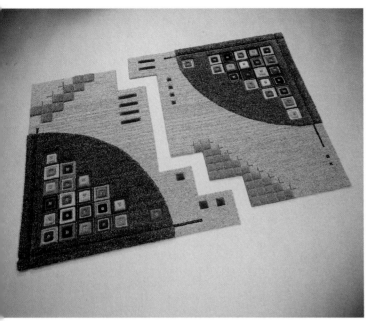

Two-part rugs like *Mixed Doubles* (1987, 54 in. by 74 in.) offer the flexibility of rearranging the individual sections to create an entirely different look. (Photo by Roger Schreiber, Seattle.)

This detail from *Mixed Doubles* shows how delicate metallic yarns can be used in functional rugs by nestling them among sculpted shapes to protect them from wear. This piece has high and low dimensional areas, with both cut and uncut pile. (Photo by Roger Schreiber, Seattle.)

and solved the potential problem of wear on that one corner.

My two-part rugs are a result of my working with paper shapes and different furniture arrangements. Fitted together, a two-part rug looks like any other rectangular shape. When separated, the two parts expand to create a larger overall size and an entirely new shape. The independent parts can be placed side by side, back to back or end to end for different effects. It takes some planning and forethought in the design process to accomplish this versatility. The design of the rug interior must be worked out carefully so the lines and shapes fit each position in which the two parts can be placed.

Nonrectangular rugs developed from my cutting out small paper shapes. I began by drawing angles on paper and creating five-sided and six-sided shapes with no two sides alike. *Raz-Ma-Taz* was my first departure from a conventional rectangular rug, and it opened the door to a whole new body of work for me. This rug was pure tongue in cheek, just wild enough to use any material in any imaginable way. It went beyond what I'd done before and offered a new sense of freedom — one that I still enjoy.

Once the basic shape of the rug is decided upon, you have to design what goes inside. Often there are too many ideas you wish to pursue, and you can't fit them all into one rug. Isolating these options to just one theme, such as the color scheme, can take some time, but I make a series of quick rough sketches until all the necessary ingredients jell into one design. As I work out a good balance of textural levels and establish the darks and lights, colors and materials, the design is tentatively planned. Sometimes colored pencils help clarify color patterns. If necessary, I make small paper cutout shapes — circles, squares, triangles or rectangles — to see inner shapes and study proportions more easily. I use anything I can to help finalize my mental image on paper, so it will not escape or be lost when needed.

Metro-Plex is a good example of a work that began by playing with paper cutouts. I keep a large assortment of shapes, all in a reduced scale, to use in planning geometric designs. By moving the forms around, it's easy to visualize good proportions and much quicker than drawing many sketches. This rug illustrates the importance of the relationship between the high and low surface levels. For example, the high shag on one side is played against the lower background surrounding it. There's also a balance of color and light, medium and dark areas, with color — such as the bright aqua or plum — used in a large area and as highlights in other sections.

Geometric designs come easiest for me, and many ideas are generated using just the ruler or paper cutouts. I can agonize over other designs for weeks, as I wait for the light of inspiration to come on. You must know what you like and, of course, recognize it when you see it. You don't have to settle on every single detail of a piece before you begin — those many small changes and decisions are what keep the hooking process interesting. But you do need to make the basic design choices of size, overall shape, color range and surface texture. Once you know the basic design is right, you're ready to move on.

Techniques for floor rugs

How and where a rug will be used determines the materials and construction it requires. There can be a great deal of difference between the wear a rug gets at a front door and beneath a coffee table, for example. Generally speaking, a good wool rug is hard to beat anywhere. I choose wool for its luxurious look and for its wearability, easy maintenance and overall superiority to other fibers for rugs. If a rug is to be placed in a kitchen, a bathroom or a doorway, consider a washable and long-wearing fiber. A tightly hooked rug in cotton or synthetics can actually improve with laundering, developing a soft, comfortable surface over time.

In selecting hooking materials, I first try to use what I have on hand. Often this means dyeing small amounts of this and that so the colors blend, but the subtle variations add to the beauty. Any odd fibers can be plied into multiple strands to serve as backgrounds or to be worked in the areas of least wear. All of this may take a little clever planning, but it's a great feeling to see inventory dwindle and be put to good use at last.

Quality of construction should always be a prime consideration. I've learned over the years that the difference between good quality and bad is usually only a pound of yarn and an ounce of

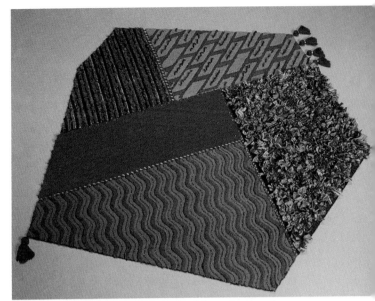

Irregular shapes can be a refreshing change from the traditional rectangular format for rugs. *Raz-Ma-Taz* (1982, 64 in. by 69 in.), the first irregularly shaped rug the author worked, includes cotton, velvet and satin yarns and cut yardage hooked in pile heights of up to 2 in. (Photo by the author.)

Geometric paper cutouts were the source of inspiration for *Metro-Plex* (1984, 72 in. by 98 in.). The rug was made from plied wools, hand-dyed and commercially dyed yarns and yardage, all designed to balance color as well as light, medium and dark areas in the work.

Before making any project, it's wise to work sample squares to establish the correct density of the hooked fiber. In these test squares, the one on the left is hooked too loosely, while that on the right is worked too densely. The square in the middle shows the correct density.

To maintain the upright pile of a high shag, hook a short filler row between rows. For clarity's sake, the filler yarn here is white, but its color should in fact be compatible with the main yarn to keep it from showing. As the left of the sample indicates, the filler row is invisible when the work is complete.

common sense (in other words, don't skimp on materials or on the time needed to plan a project). As you begin to design each project, ask yourself some basic questions. How will it wear, both now and in years to come? What will it look like when walked upon or vacuumed? Will it be washed by machine or by hand? Will it be dry cleaned? Don't forget to consider the floor. Will the rug need a pad or a double hem? What materials should be used and how? Should the stitches be close together? How far apart should the rows be? All these questions stay in my mind throughout the making of each piece.

Good construction is essential for any floor rug, and it's mandatory for a high-pile rug. Using a good-quality rug wool is a must, but the way this wool is hooked is equally important. A high shag should stand up well and not flatten out when walked upon. Most people think that this is achieved by hooking very densely. A better approach, and one that's also good if you don't want to use up a lot of expensive yarn, is to hook a filler row with less costly yarn.

Establishing the correct density of hooking for a rug takes a bit of testing. Because yarns differ in weight, I usually make a 6-in. square sample to test. I place this test square flat on the floor, step

on it and check to see if the pile stays upright. If the pile is too loose, it will flatten out and wear out quickly. If it's too dense, it will produce a surface that's stiff and uncomfortable (and it will waste yarn). Making a pile too dense is almost as bad as making one too loose. Quickly working a test sample to find the right density is well worth the time and effort.

Generally speaking, the heavier the rug yarn, the more space needed between the loops and the rows. For the heaviest yarns, loops are placed in the backing holes every two to three holes apart. Rows are ½ in. to ⅝ in. apart with a filler row in between. The shorter, lightweight yarns used for the filler row are often plied double or triple, or placed in every hole—whatever is needed to fill the row sufficiently for the right density.

To incorporate filler rows, alternate a row of good wool yarn at its highest loop with a filler row worked in a loop about half the height of the first row. The filler row is the key. It holds up the higher rug yarns, creating a denser and stronger pile. As a bonus, because these shorter loops rarely show, it's a marvelous opportunity to use up leftover yarns. The color must be compatible with the main yarn, however, since an occasional loop may peek through.

Determining quantities of materials

Determining how much fiber you need for a hooked project is difficult, especially if you try to avoid math as much as I do. There are many variables involved—loop height, weights of yarn, density of hooking and design intentions. My basic approach is to decide what to make from what I have on hand. I mix yarns and fabrics, dyeing some if necessary, and when my studio is bursting at the seams, I try to avoid making any new purchases. Even so, I usually go out and find more of some irresistible material. The key to figuring out how much yarn, yardage or other material you need—besides educated guessing based on experience—is to make a sample swatch and then do some calculations. Here's how I best determine my project needs.

When working with yarn I have on hand, I first weigh out ½ oz. (I use an antique 25-lb. scale, but a baby scale or any scale that shows ounces will work.) I then set the hooking needle to the desired loop length, decide how far apart the rows and stitches will be hooked in my design, work several inches and then measure my sample. If, for example, I am able to hook a 6-in. square from the ½ oz. of yarn, that would mean I would need 2 oz. of yarn to work 1 sq. ft. (12 in. by 12 in.). By extension, I would need 18 oz., or 1 lb. 2 oz., of yarn to hook 1 sq. yd. (3 ft. by 3 ft.).

When I order new yarns, I never trust myself. I calculate how much I think I'll need, then order more. I use the same method of figuring as above, using a similar weight of yarn to work the sample. A general rule of thumb is that, when working with heavy rug yarns with a ¾-in. pile, you'll need ½ lb. for every square foot of hooked work. Medium and lightweight yarns worked in a ¼-in. pile require 4 oz. for every square foot of hooked work.

For estimating cut yardage, I also work a test sample, which I find almost as distasteful to do as math, but it's a necessary step. To make the sample, try cutting a fabric strip ¼ in. wide by 1 yd. long. Hook this strip at the desired loop length and see how many inches of finished work you produce. Based on this and the size of the area you want to work with cut strips, you can "guesstimate" how many inches of the cut strips you'll need and, in turn, the initial size of the uncut yardage. As a general guideline, a ¼-in. strip 1 yd. long will hook 10 in. to 12 in. of finished work in a ¼-in. high loop. After some practice, you'll be able to assess the needs of a piece with fair accuracy.

When it comes to determining quantities of unusual materials, there's no general rule to follow. It's mostly guesswork. If possible, buy only a small amount and see how far it goes, then buy more. If this is impossible, buy more than you think you need at the outset. Better yet, when you find a fantastic buy, stock up. When shopping at salvage sales, remember that you'll often find these unusual materials only once. I frequently buy all I can, which explains my large inventory and my constant need for more room in my studio.

How to make a little go a long way

Extending fabric so that it fulfills the needs of a piece can sometimes be a struggle, but when a fabric in limited supply is just right, you find a way. First, go through your available supply to find all similar colors or patterns in either yarn or yardage. By mixing these in the piece, you can often end up with enough material as well as a far more interesting blend of textures and colors. For example, I'll often find four compatible blue shades to intermix equally. At a distance it just looks like an interesting blue texture, but up close, it becomes an intriguing texture, alive and with a new dimension.

Don't rely solely on mixing yardage with yardage to extend your material supply. Combine yarns with yardage, add prints to plains—the combinations work beautifully. This is a perfect time to use odds and ends that have been sitting around taking up space. It's these spontaneous mixtures that make any fiber work more challenging and interesting—not to mention the great feeling you get from using up all those misguided purchases.

There are times when you just can't figure out your needs exactly. You know you probably have enough yarn or yardage, but you feel uneasy taking the chance. When this happens to me, I leave spaces unhooked, maybe one row every 3 in. or a 1-in. void at regular intervals. These blank rows or spaces will be filled in after I finish working the section this way, or when I know I'm not running short of yarn. Once I've completed the section, I check my yarn supply. If it's plentiful, I go back and fill in the missing rows. If I discover I don't have enough yarn, I find a compatible yarn or yardage for those spaces. This can enhance the design, or sometimes the yarns or yardage can be matched so closely that the addition is not obvious.

Another no-math method of estimating your needs is to divide your supply in half, then in half again in fourths. By the time you hook one-fourth of your material, you can visually measure how far the total amount will hook. If you can tell that you'll run short, simply redesign the work to produce a very similar effect to what you originally intended.

Dyeing the fiber (see pp. 71-73) is one final alternative when materials start to dwindle. Because this adds another step to the process, it's my last resort. I usually get desperate, take material in hand and shop until I find the closest match. It's not unlike me to cut up a perfectly good dress because its color or texture is just right. I've also been known to pull a wool blanket off the bed to finish my masterpiece (we needed an electric blanket anyway).

To equalize the colors of these remnant yarns, I often throw them all into the washing machine with a package of Rit to dye them the correct color. (For details on dyeing, see pp. 71-73. If I don't have any surplus yarns to use, I fill in with inexpensive synthetics like knitting worsted, which I try to purchase on sale. I never waste precious wools or good yarns for these filler rows.

For sheer beauty and wearability, nothing compares to sculpted shapes (see pp. 66-69). If hooked properly, they never flatten out and will wear forever. The main drawback to this technique is that it is very slow to work. Try to reserve it for small areas, such as strong focal points. I usually finish the sculpted areas before moving on to work the rest of the piece. This way I test my patience to see how much I want to include in the total piece. And it's easier to design other areas like backgrounds once the main sculpted designs are completed.

Although it takes some planning, the addition of delicate fibers or metal elements often gives an exciting and unusual design dimension to functional hooked projects like rugs. Even the most fragile materials can be used in floor rugs with excellent results, but common sense must prevail. The selection of materials isn't as important as the way they are used. If you mentally picture a dimensional surface, it's easy to understand that the highest textures will take the most wear and abuse. By contrast, the very low areas of this surface will essentially never be walked upon or worn. I take advantage of this to add small amounts of delicate fibers like satins, printed cottons, Mylar and metallics. These low, fragile areas need to be kept small and must be surrounded by the higher, protective fibers.

As with fragile fibers, you must consider the necessary limitations when you add metal elements to floor rugs. Keep in mind how uncomfortable large surfaces of hooked wire loops might be to walk on, and how foot traffic would affect these areas. It is best to keep these areas small and low, with higher textures on each side for protection. Metal elements applied flat (like grommets, eyelets and washers) are usually of less concern than hooked wire, but they demand a good bond to withstand foot traffic and vacuuming. *Bear Rug*, one of my favorite pieces, combines an unusual hooking material with metal elements.

Bear Rug (1985, 60 in. by 102 in.) combines black bear fur with black cowhide suede, wool, synthetics (for structural strength and shine) and silver-colored metal washers. (Collection of Mr. and Mrs. Edward Elson, New York City; detail photograph by the author.)

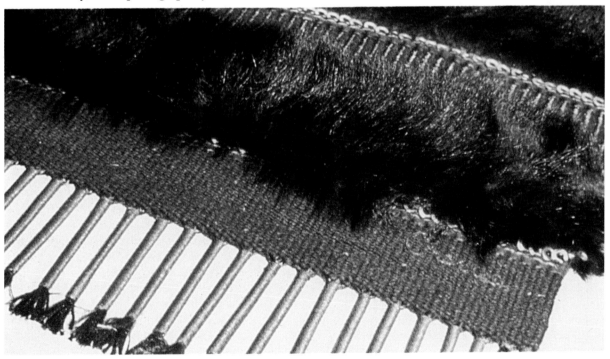

Split Decision (1986, 27 in. by 107 in.) is a two-part rug with a low, hooked background and 24 removable accent squares attached with Velcro. These accent squares can be lifted off in seconds and replaced with squares of other colors, giving the rug tremendous versatility. (Photos by Roger Schreiber, Seattle.)

Interchangeable rug parts

If you love changes as much as I do, a design innovation I've tried using might appeal to you: interchangeable rug parts. By using Velcro on the back of sections of the rug, you can change some of its parts in seconds and alter the overall design or color accents.

Velcro, the key component in this flexible design, consists of two interlocking bands, one with stiff polyester hooks, the other with soft nylon loops. This fastening material is sold at yard-goods stores by the inch or by the yard in ¾-in., 1½-in. and 2-in. widths, as well as in small packages of circles or squares. (It's often more economical to buy it by the yard in strips, although you'll find a little can last a long time.) Pressed together, Velcro's two parts form a remarkably strong bond and will remain intact until pulled apart with a sharp tug. Velcro's use has expanded phenomenally in the last few years, replacing buttons and tied laces on sportswear, shoes and many other pieces of clothing.

From the moment I first started working with Velcro, I knew this remarkable material had more to offer than just hanging works on the wall (see pp. 120-123 for installation information). *Split Decision* is a two-part rug with a light grey background and 24 removable accent squares in darker grey. These squares are attached to the rug with small strips of Velcro and can be lifted off and replaced in seconds with squares in different accent colors. When the squares are in place, the Velcro bond holds well enough to withstand foot traffic and vacuuming.

In a piece like this, of course, the design must be thought out carefully in advance so that the concept works well in the final piece. When you're planning your design, keep in mind that neutral backgrounds seem to work best, because they allow for greater variety in the color accents of the squares. Once the planning is completed, the only extra work these rugs require is making sure the measurements of the removable parts are exact and sewing on the Velcro strips. The versatility that this technique offers is open-ended. For example, you can design a rug with different color accents for seasonal changes, or, if you repaint or refurnish the room, the rug can easily take on a new life too.

Works for exhibition and public spaces

Designing pieces for exhibition or for public spaces requires a different design approach than creating work for your own environment or simply for pleasure. Exhibition work offers enormous freedom in terms of design. Any size, color, material or technique can be used. The only person you have to please is yourself.

Most of the work I enter in exhibitions has been done as a series. This has not always been intentional, but often a new piece will become a continuation of the last. A typical example is the two-part rug series. *Creme-de-la-Creme* (shown on the cover) was designed because I wanted an adjustable rug to fit a large space. This idea worked so well that I was encouraged to try another rug that assembled in more diverse ways—side by side, back to back, front to front, both together and apart. The result was *Mixed Doubles* (see the photos on p. 88), a two-part rug similar to *Creme-de-la-Creme* but worked with copper elements. Then I wanted the sectioned rug to do even more, and *Split Decision* (see the photos on the facing page) was the answer. It adjusts in so many ways that it's hard to decide which configuration to leave it in. The proportions were worked out on ¼-in. graph paper so that the two parts would work well for either a long runner or a shorter rectangle, positioned together or separated. The idea of interchangeable squares that emerged from this rug will surely set the stage for other pieces to follow.

Exhibitions are the arena that allow you the opportunity to experiment, to show and to sell. It is a chance to be completely expressive and uninhibited, and to see how your work stands in comparison to that of others. You are limited only by your own talent, technical ability and the available material.

When I create work for exhibitions, I make the pieces strong and sturdy enough to withstand handling and shipping. All pieces are latexed thoroughly, and hanging structures are designed to be stable and easy to install. I always include a detailed set of drawings and instructions, and clearly mark the installation supports so that even the most inexperienced gallery assistant can understand how the work should be hung.

To find out where to exhibit your work, check the entry listings and advertisements in leading fiber magazines (see Resources on pp. 141-145). They'll have addresses and phone numbers for application details. Since most work is juried from slides, it's important to have your work photographed in a professional manner.

Works for public spaces

Works for public spaces have entirely different design and construction requirements from residential commissions or works for exhibition. Aside from the visual significance of a piece for a public space, you must attend to the details of maintenance, security, budget and time restrictions. And instead of having the work approved by a single client, as you would for a residential commission, you may work with an architect, interior designer, owner and art committee.

The prerequisite for designing works for public spaces is common sense. It can be difficult to use common sense when you get a fantastic but somewhat impractical idea, but consider carefully how the public will interact with your work. If you're in doubt, spend some time discreetly watching your intended viewers' reactions to public art. You may be shocked to find out that the public is likely to do anything they can get away with. If vandalism and maintenance aren't strongly considered when you design the work, problems can easily arise, and marvelous materials suddenly become very vulnerable.

Security in public spaces can sometimes be good, but often it's nonexistent. Consequently, your design ingenuity must, in the worst case, prevent the work from being stolen. Strong and secure methods of installation are as critical to a piece for a public space as its aesthetic value. Yet even with the best-planned installations, things can happen. Can you imagine a 35-ft. hanging weighing 55 lb. being stolen? That was my unfortunate experience—and what a challenge for the thief! It was carelessness on my part for trusting the ground security and not checking out the area. The roof that held this hanging could be approached from an adjoining roof by any able-bodied youth—and apparently it was.

Maintenance in public buildings is often as discouraging as security. In spite of well-written instructions, an artist's offer to provide yearly inspections or other such encouragements, maintenance for public pieces is frequently mishandled or overlooked. Often the maintenance crew will clean a work with inappropriate materials or, at the other extreme, never touch it because they know it's art.

Fortunately, it's not all as bleak as it sounds. I still love the opportunity to design a piece that meets all these challenges. I work harder on better installation methods, techniques that endure and colors that won't fade, and I'm continually on the lookout for fibers that will withstand the inevitable wear and tear they will get in public spaces. The use of the monofilament surface technique (see pp. 57-59) was solely a result of making fiber works for public areas. The use of plastics, metals and foils has also definitely played an important role in this respect.

The actual design of a piece for a public space requires a basic knowledge of how to read architectural blueprints. Often these prints will be your only source of measurements, as is the case when the building is not yet completed or is located across the country. In addition to blueprints, a color board should be requested indicating materials for surrounding flooring, paint, carpeting and furniture. You can then present a scale drawing or scale model with samples of your ideas. This proposal is submitted for review to the selection committee, which may, in turn, ask for some revisions in your plans before granting final approval of the project. Your proposal must clearly show exactly what you'll be submitting. Even when the selection committee has reviewed slides and photos of your past work, they'll not want any surprises—nor will you—once the piece is installed. Thus the more you can find out about the space for which you're designing, and the more the selection committee can find out about what you're planning, the more successful your "collaboration" will be. After all your efforts, you'll find that there's nothing quite like walking into the building and seeing your work hung in a central spot of honor for all to appreciate.

Designing wall hangings, wearables and upholstery

After working within the constraints of rug design, the increased flexibility that comes with designing wall hangings is enjoyable. With wall works, the main emphasis is on visual impact. Decisions will be based on what the piece will do for the space rather than on concerns about construction, wearability and materials.

When designing works for a private residence or your own home, you'll face the fewest restrictions. The work can be proportioned to fit the given space, and color schemes are usually predetermined by the surroundings, leaving design, techniques and materials as open options.

I've never fully understood why, but I usually know immediately what type of wall piece I want to hang in a given space. This spontaneous image results from a mixture of past experience and a longtime interest in and attention to fiber, interior design and architecture. When this first impression strikes, it's rare that I change my mind later.

Of course, there are other times when I'm not this lucky, when that "great image" is just not there. Then it's back to the drawing board to make countless rough sketches, study measurements and persevere. The inspiration may be slow in coming, but eventually the design emerges.

Impressions was designed for a sophisticated interior of subtle greys, with accents of plum, blue-grey and wine. The serenity of this living-dining area called for an unassuming, textured wall. The large wall hanging encompasses most of the wall in the dining area, but because of its use of soft grey monotones, does not overpower the viewer.

When I'm working on such large-scale projects, the one thing that keeps it exciting for me is adding at least one new element, technique or material. In this piece, for example, I found the first opportunity to use a wonderful silver wire as a hooking material. A double strand of wire forms the 1-in. diagonal lines, which reflect in selected areas as the light catches the surface. A combination of technique and textures keeps the overall design quietly changing. Using a float mounting, which hangs the work 2 in. away from the wall (see pp. 120-123) gives the work a sense of depth and accentuates the pierced cutout edge detailing (also a new style for me).

Impressions **(1985, 73 in. by 93 in.) is a wall piece commissioned by Mr. and Mrs. Roland M. Trafton of Seattle. By combining a palette of soft greys with textural interest, the artist created a design that integrates with its environment. The work includes mixed yarns and cut yardage, with accents of silver wire.**

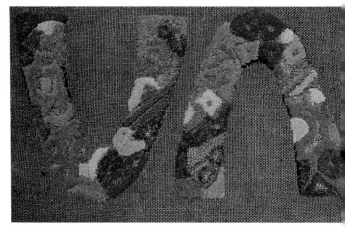

After years of trying to describe the type of fiber work she does, the author created this hooked vest in 1984 to wear to exhibition previews and let it do the explaining. The vest is hooked in sculpted wools and shiny synthetics on a black burlap backing. Unhooked areas of the backing were machine-quilted to equalize the stiffness.

The hooked shoes at top, created in 1989, were worked in sculpted wools with beading, a velour lining and leather soles. Each shoe was hooked in a single piece on the canvas (above) and seamed at the center back. The author devised the pattern based on a pair of her own slippers. (Photo above by the author.)

Hooked wearables

If hooked textures can be great in rugs and wall hangings, why not in wearables? Consider making jackets, vests, hats, shoes, boots, bags and accessories — all hooked with wonderful textures, patterns and colors.

Most of the techniques used in rugs or wall hangings can be easily adapted to work in wearable garments or accessories. There are a few things to keep in mind, however, as you begin to design a wearable. Unlike working with fabric yardage, you cannot simply complete a few yards

of hooking and then cut and stitch the garment. You must decide upon the style, pattern, hooking design and techniques to be used all before you begin, and then you must hook each section of the garment to fit each pattern part exactly.

The first thing to consider is the style of the garment or accessory relative to the stiffness that results from hooking. If the item is something that needs to be flexible, like a jacket, you must plan to hook with lightweight wools or in small areas so the entire backing is not covered. If you want to hook more densely, consider hooking a hat or bag.

Next, carefully select the pattern. Choose one with simple lines and as few seams as possible. Think about how many seams you can eliminate from the garment. For example, if the side or shoulder seams can be joined and the pattern will still remain flat on the backing material, it will save you time and trouble later.

An exact pattern and fit should be worked out before the first stitch is hooked. If you're using a new pattern, pin the seams to check the fit or, better still, make a muslin pattern. After fitting and making any necessary alterations on the muslin or paper pattern, transfer the pattern to heavy unprinted newsprint or kraft paper. Cut off any seam allowances that may be on the original commercial pattern. They will not be part of the hooking area and will only cause confusion as you're working. You'll also want to avoid hooking in the seam areas, since the sewing machine will not be able to stitch through densely hooked areas. (Later, when the piece is finished, you'll cut it out of the larger backing-material area, leaving space for seam allowances for stitching and assembly.) Mark the newsprint pattern clearly to indicate where parts are to line up.

Select the backing material for wearables carefully since it will be used for underlying structure as well as design purposes. If you want a more flexible garment, consider leaving parts of the backing unhooked as a background and letting some of the backing show. If the backing is to be seen, I use a good-quality burlap or linen. The variety of colors available in burlap works well for vests, jackets or belts. If you're creating less flexible items, like boots, bags, hats or belts, consider covering the surface with sculpted shapes.

Pin the paper pattern to your backing material, which should already be stretched taut on your frame. Make sure the pattern aligns with the grain of the fabric if necessary. With indelible pen or contrasting pencil, trace the outline of the pattern exactly, marking any notches or construction indications. Leave a space of ⅝ in. to 1 in. around each pattern piece to provide for seam allowances.

If there are any hooking designs to be followed on the garment, trace them from the paper draft onto the backing with dressmaker's tracing paper. The carbon transfer lines are frequently faint, so retrace them with an indelible pen if necessary

When making wearables created from hooked work, you can use a commercial pattern as the basis for the garment. Simple shapes with few seams or darts work best.

The newsprint pattern, traced from a commercial pattern, is pinned and traced onto the backing material, leaving at least a 1-in. margin around the perimeter for seam allowances. The pattern is carefully aligned with the grain and positioned so that the hooking area fully clears the frame. In this photo, the author is using white pencil for tracing and marking notches so they will show up on the black backing.

(see the photos on pp. 104-106). The pen lines will not show after the work is completed.

Once you have completed the hooking, clip off the excess yarn ends and seal them with latex (see pp. 112-113 for a full description). If stiffness will not be a problem, lightly latex the backing of the entire garment (but not the seam allowances). If the piece must be flexible, cover only the hooked yarns or threads with latex. Use a thinned water-soluble, flexible adhesive and a small paintbrush to spread the solution. Allow the adhesive to dry overnight. Before removing the work from the frame, apply a light coat of a diluted white-glue solution to the seam allowances to prevent raveling after they're cut (see also pp. 27-28 for details on preventing edges from raveling).

After the glue solution has been allowed to dry, cut the garment for sewing, remembering to leave ⅝ in. to 1 in. for seam allowances. Sew the item by machine using a zipper foot, following the original marked pen lines and avoiding all hooked areas. If the garment has to be lined, cut the lining from the same pattern and construct it using traditional lining techniques.

If hooking wearable works intrigues you, consider the marvelous possibilities of adding beading, embroidery, applied ribbon, stitchery, metal elements or other embellishments. These possibilities can keep you at work for years.

Hooked upholstery

Hooked fabric just begs to be used for upholstery. You can't ask for a more stunning covering for chair cushions, floor or sofa pillows, loveseats or footstools. Imagine the flair that just one chair covered in these sensational textures and delicious colors brings to a room. As a bonus, these surfaces wear like floor rugs.

When designing for upholstery, ask yourself the same kind of questions you posed for rugs or wearables. Where will the work be used? How will it be seen? Must it be flexible in order to accommodate the contours of a piece of furniture, or can it be stiff? As with other hooked projects, considerations of color, size, shape, style, textures and materials all remain important.

Undoubtedly, the longest-wearing hooking technique for upholstery is sculpted forms, but don't make the mistake I did, of overdoing the

This antique rocker, worked in 1962, has a 30-in. sq. hooked seat cushion of overall sculpted shapes. The trimming process took four weeks to complete, but the hooking has held up well for many years in an active family setting.

trimming. Remember the antique rocker I mentioned in Chapter 2? Beautiful, yes, but the chair would have been just as effective if I had used half the cut work combined with a faster background technique. And it wouldn't have taken four weeks of trimming and countless blisters.

These days I use more sensible and faster techniques for pillow backs, chair seats and other flat surfaces. One approach is to cover the backing surface completely, using the shortest loop with any design or color you like. Another option is to leave some areas of the backing material exposed so that it becomes part of the color and pattern. Of course, the backing material must be of a suitable color and texture for the latter to work. Using either of these two approaches for the background,

Working from sketches to full-scale cartoons

Pillows—these were worked between 1963 and 1989—are good projects if you are just starting to hook, because they allow you to experiment with color, materials and techniques on a manageable scale. (Photo by Roger Schreiber, Seattle.)

you can easily add pattern and design to the surface, but with only half the amount of hooking time and materials you would need to cover the entire piece with sculpted effects.

Pillows are a good choice for beginning projects, because they are small enough to handle easily and are not too overwhelming. I've seen some elegant "sampler" pillows that showcase a variety of techniques and materials. Uncut loop surfaces are the fastest of all techniques. This is nice for backgrounds, but I find it hard to give up the temptation of those more tedious sculpted forms. Any of the hooking techniques work well, but good judgment must be used to keep the yarns or yardage, as well as the techniques, soundly related to the way the article will be used.

Ideas for my hooked projects often originate from sketches on scraps of paper or backs of envelopes. When I've finally decided that it's time to move beyond these sketches and doodles, I get out the "good" paper, which is actually large pieces of newsprint. It's such a relief finally to settle on an idea and go forward with it that this cartoon process is a joy.

For any work that measures under 4 ft. or 5 ft. when finished, I work directly from the rough sketch to the cartoon, that is, the full-scale paper pattern. The cartoon serves as a preparatory drawing, giving me a good idea of the actual size of the finished work and of how proportions, scale, patterns and textures may work out. I use newsprint for the cartoon. Readily available in end rolls from the local newspaper, newsprint is 28 in. wide, unprinted and inexpensive. To measure the paper, I roll it out on the floor if the project is large. When the project is larger than the paper, I tape the edges of two or more pieces together.

First, I determine the actual shape and size of the piece. Next, I fold under any excess edges of paper to fit the shapes I have in mind—I fold rather than cut the shapes to reinforce their edges—and then settle on the main design shapes and divisions. Rather than drawing a lot of confusing pencil lines, I first lay down sticks, dowels or yardsticks in the basic outline of the piece to visualize how the proportions fit into the space. Once I'm happy with the silhouette, I draw the lines on paper with a pencil, using a yardstick or straightedge as a guide. Any curved lines are lightly sketched at this stage; they will be darkened when the design decisions are final.

How detailed and intricate you make the cartoon is up to you. I prefer to indicate only the major proportions and work out the squares, circles or patterns on the actual fiber work. This approach works for me because many of my pieces are quite large and abstract, and rely on textures and grid for pattern. The patterns and designs often evolve as the work progresses. By contrast, some people feel more comfortable knowing where each design element will be on the finished work and therefore want to include them in the paper cartoon, which is fine. When the cartoon is finished, I note the colors, pile heights, textures and any new ideas or materials to be tried.

For projects that are larger than 5 ft., I often create a reduced-scale drawing, model or architectural rendering to give me a better idea of what I want to do before proceeding to the cartoon. It's easier to get a sense of overall proportions and design in reduced scale than it is with a massive paper drawing. If these small 4-in. to 6-in. drawings are well designed and true to scale, they'll be just as proportionately correct when enlarged, no matter what their eventual size.

To determine the scale of proportion to use for a reduced-scale drawing, I check the ruler to see what size fits best on my drawing paper. The scale can be ⅛ in. to 1 ft., ½ in. to 1 ft., or any other proportion that fits the paper. The determining factor (in addition to your paper size) is that the drawing must be large enough to indicate all the information you need as an exact guideline. If, for example, I decided that ½ in. equaled 1 ft. on a 10-ft. by 10-ft. sq. piece, I would count out ten ½-in. marks on my ruler (a total of 5 in.) and draw lines this length to represent the four sides of the square. I would proceed similarly with all the measurements for the piece, keeping in mind that each ½ in. visually represented 1 ft. Graph paper can be very helpful in creating a scale drawing, since the individual squares are usually ¼ in. on a side, which makes measurement much easier.

Once I've decided on my scale, I try to copy what I drew in my rough sketch, rendering it in proportion and more detail. All design flaws become more apparent at this stage, since the drawing is now more than a fuzzy mental image. As

An accurately proportioned scale drawing lets you refine your design. For large works, this is an important intermediate step between rough sketches and the final paper cartoon. Here, the author creates a scale drawing from preliminary sketches for *Mixed Doubles* (see the top photo on p. 88 for the finished work).

with the full-scale cartoon, the overall size and shape of the scale drawing is established first; then the major areas of line and design, like proportion, focal points, shapes and forms, are filled in. I never rush this stage, because I know I'll be using these measurements for a long time to come. I rearrange the lines until I'm completely satisfied, and then I double-check my math for accuracy.

After a satisfactory scale drawing is completed, a full-scale cartoon for the piece can be made. This cartoon drawing for the larger work is created in the same way as the small ones mentioned above, only this time the measurements are taken directly off the scale drawing. To create the full-scale cartoon, use newsprint, rolling out approximate lengths and taping together a sufficient number of widths to give you the dimension needed. Working out the contour of irregularly shaped pieces takes a bit of doing, but you can again use the rods, dowels or yardsticks to indicate and mark any angles. After establishing the outside shape, I measure each design section accurately with a yardstick, translate the reduced measurements into full-scale dimensions and draw them on the large cartoon. For example, if I used a scale of ½ in. to 1 ft. in my scale drawing and the drawing showed a section 1¼ in. long, I would draw this line as 2½ ft. on the large cartoon.

Once all the major lines have been drawn, I fold the outside edges under so I can see exactly what this "masterpiece" is going to look like. I take time to study the cartoon closely at this stage. If it's a floor rug, I leave it on the floor and scrutinize the proportions from every side. I then stand on a high stool, which gives me a new perspective. If it's a wall hanging, I pin the cartoon on my studio wall to imagine the work in its finished position. If possible, I place the cartoon in the location for which the work is designed to give me a final critical view.

It's important to label the final cartoon clearly for quick and easy reference before the design is transferred to the backing. You'll find that during the work stage, many measurements can be confused and countless ideas forgotten unless you have clear indications of the piece's height, width, exact overall size, the date these measurements were arrived at and the work's title, if any. Also indicate the dark and light areas for good balance,

A full-size paper cartoon is created on unprinted newsprint by enlarging the measurements from the scale drawing and using wooden dowels to help visualize the final shape. The cartoon becomes the full-size paper pattern that will later be transferred to the backing.

Selecting fibers and colors for the work is often done by placing yarn skeins and cones right on the finished cartoon. With the full-sized paper pattern cut out and accurately marked before you, it's easy to visualize what materials are needed for specific sections of the work.

and the textures and pile levels of high and low hooked areas. Sometimes I note the colors, but usually I prefer to sort them out later by stacking yarns and remnants on top of the cartoon. In addition, I always mark the top, center and wrong side of the cartoon, a step which saves time and mental energy when transferring the paper pattern to the backing. If I'm using geometric patterns, diagonals or horizontals, I also draw up and down directional markings at this time.

I save all my sketches, scale drawings and cartoons from each project. Any models I make also stay in my possession. This has been one of the wisest decisions I've ever made. These cartoons are like dress patterns. You know how they fit and work, and you can refer back to them, often duplicating a similar shape or size. You know the proportions have already been worked out to your satisfaction, and you don't have to spend energy rethinking those decisions. Although I prefer to create one-of-a-kind pieces and rarely duplicate my work, a few of my clients have had pieces stolen and later requested identical pieces to replace them. Protest as I may, the owner or architect very often wants exactly the same thing back in place. So I have recreated them. And what a godsend it is to have the entire design, measurements and details all at hand. It is, without a doubt, the only consolation of having to do a work completely over again.

Transferring the design to the backing

Once the paper cartoon has been made and the backing is stretched on the frame, the design is transferred as accurately as possible. There are several different transfer methods, and each differs depending on the size, scale and type of design, that is to say, whether it's geometric or freeform. My transfer method is just the opposite of what many people do. They trace the design on the backing before the fabric is stretched on the frame, but this has never made sense to me. An accurate transfer is all but impossible when drawing on a limp piece of cloth that wiggles and moves every time it's touched. On the frame, the backing is taut and firm, and the transfer is much more precise. This approach has worked so well for me that I recommend it as the best way to get a reliable and exact transfer.

The cartoon is pinned to the stretched backing for transfer. Space for hems and hooking has been left on all sides, and the pattern has been checked to make sure it aligns with the grain of the backing. The excess fabric rolled at both top and right frame edges offers protection from tack stripping.

The markings from the cartoon are carefully transferred to the backing material using an indelible marking pen and a yardstick as a guide. It's best to avoid overdrawing on the canvas, since too many lines can cause confusion.

With the cartoon transferred to the backing, the author stitches the work's outline using the speed needle set on a short loop with a yarn that contrasts with the backing. This keeps the design visible from both sides, and any misalignments of the backing on the grain can be easily seen and quickly corrected.

With any design, first establish the outline. Keep in mind that you'll be working on the reverse side of the finished piece, so make sure you reverse the design by turning it over when transferring it. For regular or geometric shapes, I often transfer just the measurements, marking the dimensions with pins. A soft pencil or indelible pen can be used to connect the lines. I often "draw" these lines with my speed needle in a short loop with any yarn I have handy (and which can be taken out later). This gives me an immediate indication of the outline on both sides of the canvas, and shows me if everything is on grain. It is crucial to correct anything off grain at this point by restretching the backing, since even the slightest deviation will cause other problems later on.

Once the outline has been established in a geometric piece, I measure the distances between shapes and transfer these to the backing. In order to follow the cartoon accurately, I measure precisely to one-sixteenth of an inch. I use a yardstick for this part, since it rests flat on the backing and is much easier to manipulate and more accurate than a cloth measuring tape. To transfer diagonal lines, mark the two corner points and draw a clean straight line connecting them with a permanent pen and yardstick. Use a medium-tipped marking pen rather than one with a wide tip for marking more precise measurements.

After all the main lines, shapes and proportions have been drawn, I hook with yarn over any pen lines to keep the design visible from each side at all times. Once good proportions have been worked out on the paper cartoon and transferred exactly, these outlines are followed until the work is completed. I allow a great deal of flexibility in techniques, colors or materials within these outline shapes, but the overall outline design remains fixed as I had it on paper.

As you transfer your design to the backing, avoid overdrawing. One thing most of us can't resist is drawing like crazy all over this nice clean space. When I first started, I ended up with so many lines and colors that after a while, I wouldn't know which line to follow. I now draw as little as possible on the backing, and prefer to make lines in yarn rather than pen or pencil whenever possible. With the speed needle, you quickly hook a line, and if you're not satisfied, simply pull the yarn out and restitch it, without leaving an unerasable mess.

When transferring irregular shapes, I find that the easiest approach is to pin the paper cartoon right on the backing. It's easy to center the shape

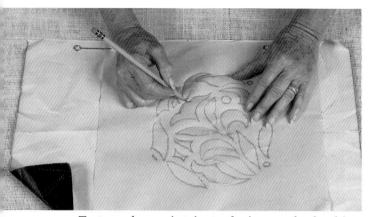

To transfer an intricate design to the backing material, use dressmaker's tracing paper placed between the original design and the backing. Since the pattern will be transferred to the wrong side of the finished work, make sure to reverse the image by turning it over before tracing it.

Making projects larger than the frame

Ideally, hooking projects should be 2 in. smaller than the frames that hold them while they're being hooked. But things never seem to end up that way for me since my eye tends to see everything on a slightly larger scale than I've drawn. So, in order to keep my options open and be able to design a bit more as I hook, most of the time I work on a piece in sections, even when I'm using a 7-ft. frame. This way I complete one section at a time, remove it from the frame, move the next section to be worked into place, restretch the canvas on the frame and begin to hook again.

This process seems to confuse people more than any other process in hooking, but it's really quite simple. If you follow a few important guidelines, you'll have professional joins that only you and your hooking tool will ever know about. Even when I've worked a piece in many sections, I can never tell where these sections begin and end once the piece is completed.

Start with backing material large enough to complete the entire work. Be sure to figure in the overall measurements of the piece, and an allowance for hems and for fully covering the frame when the piece is stretched on it (see p. 22 for information on determining the amount of backing material). Stretch the first section — generally a lower corner or side of the piece — on the frame in the usual manner (see pp. 28-31 for information on stretching the canvas). Roll up all excess backing material evenly and tightly. Pin this roll on top of the exposed tack stripping, if you're using it, or close to the frame if you're using thumbtacks. Transfer the design from the cartoon for this stretched section, as described on pp. 104-106. Work this section completely, stopping just before hooking the edge that will continue into the next section. This edge will be worked with the move in mind, hooked in zigzag fashion to keep from creating a noticeable ridge or seam along the edge.

To ensure that the join will not show, leave long yarn tails (12 in. or more) at the end of the rows hooked in zigzag fashion. These ends will be rethreaded and hooked into the next section after

within the frame, then mark the main design shapes. For large curved forms, circles or irregular shapes, I cut separate paper patterns in newsprint, pin these in place on the backing and then draw around them with pen or pencil. Using a template like a plate or saucer to trace the circles makes it an easier task.

If, however, a very intricate pattern must be followed, I use dressmaker's tracing paper. This material, which is not to be confused with typing carbon, is available at any yardage or sewing outlet in convenient colors, ranging from white, yellow and orange to red and blue. The package contains sheets of each color; you can decide which shows best on your backing color. To trace accurately with the backing on the frame may seem a bit tricky, but it's not. Place the frame on a table or floor with the hooking side up. Lay several books or any firm base beneath the backing to support the fabric, providing a solid surface for tracing. Lay the transfer paper carbon-side down on the hooking side of the backing, with the design to be transferred on top of it. *Remember to reverse the design,* since you're tracing on the wrong side of the finished work. Using a blunt tool and steady pressure, trace the design, transferring it to the backing. If the carbon does not transfer clearly, darken the lines afterwards with a pencil or indelible marking pen.

the canvas is repositioned on the frame (see the section on reversed threading on p. 109). Meanwhile, these long dangling ends should be tucked inside the rolled backing or pinned to one side out of the way until you're ready to move the section.

After each section is completed, finish it in the usual way by clipping the yarn ends and applying latex to the backing, up to 2 in. from the unfinished edge (see pp. 112-113). Make sure you don't latex any of the next area to be worked, since it will become too stiff and difficult to hook through. Leave this section on the frame until the latex dries, usually overnight.

Before removing the finished section from the frame, measure and mark exactly, two or three key points in the design by making small dots or lines with the marking pen on both the backing and the paper cartoon. These dots will serve as important registration marks that will enable you to align the pattern accurately as you reposition and stretch the next section on the frame.

Remove the completed section from the frame. If you're using tack stripping on the frame, carefully place the edge with the finished hooking over the tacks so they won't snag your completed work. Move the backing so that the next section to be hooked covers nearly all the frame. That is, if the unfinished edge was on the left of the first section hooked, it will now become the right edge of the new section being worked. In repositioning the canvas, make sure to place this unfinished edge at least 2 in. away from the frame so it can be hooked without interference from the frame. Stretch the latexed edge of this finished section taut as you secure it to the frame, anchoring it with metal pushpins hammered in every 2 in. Try to use pushpins with long shafts so they'll accommodate the thickness of the hooking.

Stretch and secure the remaining three sides of the backing in the usual manner, making sure to keep the straight of the grain aligned with the frame. Place the paper cartoon over the new section, matching the registration marks precisely. Mark or measure the exact outline of the remaining design to be completed. Also transfer any necessary measurements or designs.

In the new section, first hook the long dangling yarns on the zigzag edge. Using the reversed threading method outlined on p. 109 to get started,

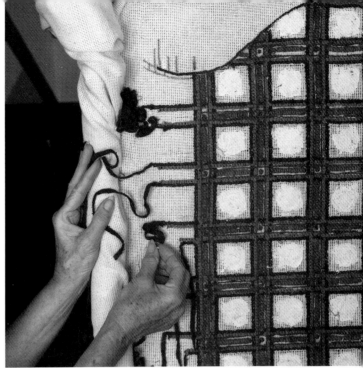

1 When hooking a piece larger than the frame, work in sections. Hook the first section, leaving a zigzag edge with long yarn ends at the edge of the frame. These yarn ends will be rethreaded and hooked once the piece is repositioned on the frame; the zigzag edge will camouflage the seam.

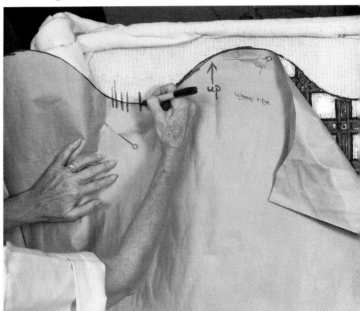

2 Before removing the completed section from the frame, check the registration marks again for alignment. Add more marks, if necessary, so that you can align the next section properly.

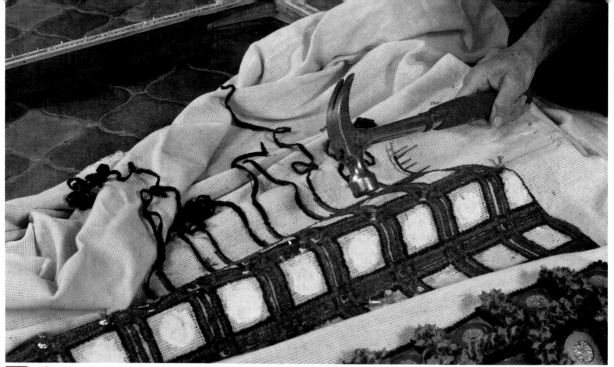

3 After removing the completed section, the next section is prepared for stretching. The zigzag edge, formerly on the left edge of the frame, now moves to the right edge. It is attached to the frame with metal pushpins, which are usually hammered in place.

4 The new section is stretched on the frame. The loose yarn ends left from the first section are ready for hooking. The new area is positioned away from the frame's edge (indicated by the pushpins) so the frame won't interfere with hooking.

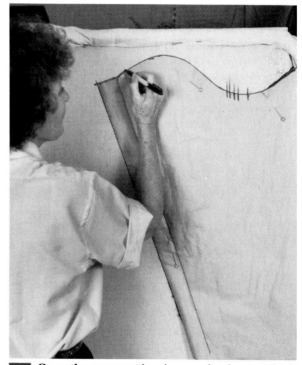

5 Once the new section is completely stretched, the design is transferred to the backing from the paper cartoon, which has been aligned with the registration marks on the canvas. Once the paper cartoon is removed, the hooking continues.

hook each of the yarns in the appropriate patterns and techniques to continue the design. (I keep a notebook with detailed directions for each project to refer back to them when needed. These notations are especially helpful when there is a long interval between moving sections.) Finish this section as the cartoon indicates, and if another section is to be hooked, work a zigzag edge, leaving long yarn tails, and begin the process again. When moving a section, if a finished area looks flattened out from being pinned to the frame, leave it for a few hours. It will usually spring back, but if it doesn't, lightly steam it with an iron, holding the iron slightly away from the hooked surface.

You can move as many sections as you want to arrive at any desired size. The largest project I ever did was a 9½-ft. circular rug on a 40-in. by 30-in. frame. That piece took 14 moves to complete. In this case, there were always two sides with zigzag edges to be continued. They were placed so that the rows were staggered and the hooking could be picked up by rethreading the long ends.

If followed carefully, this method is foolproof. Once completed, the joins are so well camouflaged that they can't be detected — and people will wonder how you ever hooked something so large without seaming.

Reversed threading

Reversed threading simply means threading the needles backward. It is usually done to pick up previously hooked yarn ends and to continue hooking with them without cutting or tying. To reverse-thread your hooking needle, take the end of the yarn, place it first in the eye or tip of the needle and run it back through the upper eye or ring. For easier threading, use a fine looped wire threader to pull the yarn or fabric strips through the needle eye (see the photos at right for a detailed explanation). Pull any excess yarn back through the needle until you reach the last stitch of hooking. With the excess yarn now pulled to the back of the needle, you can continue hooking in the usual manner.

I use reversed threading almost as much as regular threading. It avoids cutting yarns and starting over, and it's fast and easy. It's also great when you change your mind, rip something out and want to back up and begin again.

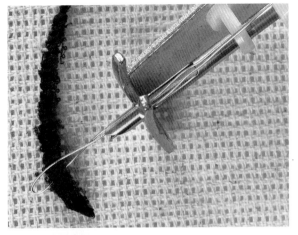

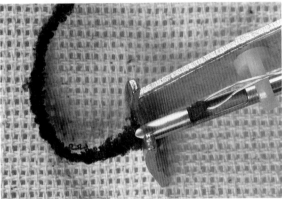

In reversed threading, the yarn is pulled back through the needle's eye from the needle's tip, just the reverse of the way it's normally threaded. This threading is used to continue working with yarn ends that have pulled out of the hooking or that you have left at the zigzag edge of a section of a large piece being worked in sections. To reverse-thread the speed needle, use a loop of bent wire slipped through the needle eye. Catch the yarn tail in the loop, pull the tail and all the excess yarn gently back through the needle, reposition the needle and keep hooking until the yarn runs out.

4

Finishing and Installation

Once the actual hooking is completed, you're about 90% of the way through your project. But the final 10% — finishing the back and installing the work — is a very important part of the process. The techniques for sealing the backing and making hems are similar for all hooked pieces, though wearables and upholstery are completed with slight variations on the basic process of finishing rugs and wall hangings because of their different uses.

Once all hooking has been completed, clip off the excess yarn ends close to the backing surface, first with large scissors (top), then with small embroidery shears. Vacuum the surface to remove all clippings. When you've finished all the clipping, apply a coat of latex to the back of the hooked area to seal the fibers and bond them to the backing (above). Keep the latex out of the hem allowance to prevent difficulty in sewing.

Finishing rugs and wall hangings

I apply a latex finish to the back of every hooked project I make. I like the way it locks the fibers in place and keeps them from pulling out. Latex helps the work retain its shape and makes rugs skidproof. It also adds a finishing touch to a piece, demonstrates a high standard of workmanship and ensures protection from wear and tear.

That's not to say that latexing the back of a piece is mandatory. If you're making a wall hanging that will never leave your living room, there's no need to go to the trouble of finishing the piece with latex. Bear in mind that the antique hooked rugs we cherish today were made hundreds of years before latexing was invented. When deciding whether to apply latex, consider how the piece will be handled, cleaned and used. If the loops are hooked firmly together, preferably worked in a low pile and left uncut, they should wear just fine without the latex finish. Nonetheless, because of the wear and inevitable need for cleaning, I always latex the back of my rugs.

If you do decide to apply latex, which is available at carpet-supply stores, the most important thing to remember is to leave the piece on the frame. Many people latex after removing the piece from the frame, but I've never found this as successful as applying the latex while the work is stretched taut. Why struggle with the frustration of a limp, uncontrollable piece of backing whose edges are always rolling in on you? On the frame, the piece remains flat and easy to work with.

To prepare for the latex application, clip all loose ends close to the backing surface or poke them through to the right side of the piece. I vacuum both the front and back of the piece using the air nozzle without any attachments. This removes any fuzz and excess threads. Place the frame (with the wrong side up) in a horizontal position, either on a table, on the floor or propped between stools or sawhorses. Make sure the room is well ventilated, because latex fumes can be noxious.

Latex comes ready to use and is always applied in nondiluted form. Pour about ½ cup to 1 cup of latex directly onto the hooked loops in the center

After the back of the hooked area has been coated with latex, any hem allowances are stiffened with a solution of diluted white glue to make them easier to handle during the construction of the piece and to keep them from raveling.

of the piece, away from the edge. Using a small metal spatula or a hard plastic knife, spread the latex evenly from the center out toward the edges. Don't use brushes for this step—you'll only ruin them. My favorite application tool is a firm plastic knife (the kind you get in a fast-food restaurant), which allows good control for applying latex at the edges.

Make sure to cover only the hooked loops with latex, not the hem. On large rugs, complete about a 2-ft. section at time, working in a regular progression from end to end. Since latex starts to dry clear in about 30 minutes, make sure you're working systematically. If you apply latex randomly to different parts of the piece, you'll have difficulty seeing which areas you've covered and which you have not once the latex starts drying.

The latex should be a surface coating, forming an even, continuous bond over the loops; one coat is sufficient. It's not advisable to saturate the fiber, nor is it necessary to work the latex deep into the loops. If you are hooking a project larger than the frame, you will be hooking in sections (see pp. 106-109). After each section is completed, clip the yarn ends and latex the back of the section be-

fore removing the work from the frame and moving on to start the next section.

To clean your hands and the spreading tool, simply roll the rubbery latex off as it dries. Because latex is very permanent, remove any excess while it's wet, using cold water if necessary.

Hems

Immediately after applying the latex, you'll need to size the backing edges to make hemming easier. This technique, one of the many I discovered while experimenting with adhesives, keeps even the flimsiest materials looking crisp and professional, and prevents them from raveling.

Using a diluted white-glue solution of 1 tablespoon of glue to 1 cup of water, spread the mixture with a 2-in. brush over the unhooked edges that will become the hem. (One cup of solution is enough to cover the hem of a rug about 3 ft. square.) Cover an area 5 in. to 7 in. wide, extending out from the hooking edge. Allow the sizing and the latex to dry on the frame completely, generally overnight. When the sizing and latex are dry, carefully take the work off the frame and use a seam ripper or razor blade to remove any exten-

After the work has been taken off the frame, remove any backing extensions (the darker fabric in the photo) with a seam ripper or razor blade

A mitered corner is created by evenly folding the backing inward. Here, the author adjusts the amount of the inner fold and its position to produce a symmetrical corner.

sion pieces that you had to add in order to stretch the backing on the frame. Save these extensions for possible reuse with future projects.

There are two basic choices of hems for rugs and wall hangings: a plain turned hem or an applied canvas-backed hem. A plain turned hem uses the actual backing fabric for the hem material. If you've used a lightweight backing material, a 6-in. hem allowance will create a 3-in. doubled hem. Heavier backing may be left single thickness and trimmed to create a 3-in. hem. Because the backing has been sized, it holds its shape, doesn't ravel and creases easily by hand.

To create a plain turned hem, fold the edge of the backing under evenly. (For a single-hem thickness, turn the edge under ½ in.) At the corners, press the folds of the hem into a mitered corner (as shown in the photo below left), cutting away any excess fabric from the interior of the miter, if necessary. (If you don't want to use a mitered corner, you can make a square corner with overlapped edges.) When the hem is folded evenly and completely, apply Tacky Glue with a brush, covering both the inside of the turned hem and the hooked edge. Press the hem edge firmly in place by hand, pulling it toward the center of the work so that none of the backing shows on the finished side.

The adhesive will grab fast enough to hold the hem in place, but not well enough for a permanent seal. For a more secure bond, the hem edges must be weighted immediately after you finish gluing. To do so, turn the rug over on the floor (protected with a sheet of plastic) so that the finished side is up. Check to make certain all parts of the hem are folded under in the proper position with the mitered or overlapped corners in place. Keeping the rug flat and even on the floor, walk on top of the piece around its edge to anchor the hem. Now weight the hem with stacks of magazines or books to ensure a good bond. Allow the hem to dry overnight in this position. Any crushed loops will spring back, or can be restored using the vacuum cleaner.

A plain turned hem is used to finish most hooked pieces, but if the backing is thin or unsightly or if a sturdy edge is needed for a rug in a high-traffic area, a canvas-backed hem is used. This hem is created by sewing a separate canvas strip to the finished work at the hooked edge, which is then turned back and secured with glue in the same way as a plain turned hem. To make this hem for shapes with straight edges, use a piece of canvas 4 in. wide, cut on the grain or at the selvage. For a circular work, use a 4-in. canvas strip cut on the bias. In both cases, turn under each side of the canvas strip ½ in. from the edge and press it flat with an iron. Sew this canvas strip to the rug as close as possible to the hooked edge, using a straight machine stitch with a zipper foot. If the rug is too large or unwieldy to fit on the sewing machine, hand-stitch the canvas close to the hooked edge, making sure your stitches don't show on the finished side. (If you've been careless with your latex application, you'll discover how difficult it is to sew by hand or machine through a latexed area.) Once the outer edge has been sewn, secure the hem with Tacky Glue, then weight it with books and magazines, as you would for a plain turned hem.

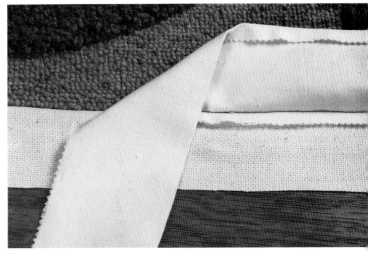

A canvas-backed hem gives a rug a more finished look. To make this hem, cut a 4-in. wide strip of canvas on the straight grain and turn under ½ in. on each edge. Then sew one folded edge to the right side of the finished piece and as close as possible to the edge of the hooking.

To bond the hem, the author spreads adhesive on the latex-coated backing and the underside of the hem edge. She will pull the hem firmly toward the center of the hooked piece to prevent the edge of the canvas from showing on the finished side.

After applying adhesive to the hem, the author weights the edge of the piece with books and magazines to ensure a strong bond and leaves it to dry overnight. (The floor is protected with a sheet of plastic.)

Once the latex coating and sizing have dried on the carpet bag, the pieces are cut out, leaving ample seam allowances for construction. Shown above are the front and side panels of the carpet bag.

Finishing wearables and upholstery

Wearables, accessories and upholstery are finished in much the same way as rugs and wall works, but care must be taken to keep the pieces functional. For garments, this means that latex application should not be too heavy, or the garment will be too stiff to wear. Hooked pieces used for upholstery, such as chair cushions, floor and sofa pillows, loveseats and footstools, must also remain flexible and functional. For any works to be stitched by machine, latex must be kept out of the seam allowances.

Once you've completed the hooking for a wearable, prepare the piece for stitching. While the piece is still on the frame, clip the loose ends and vacuum them from the piece. For minimum stiffness, apply a light coat of undiluted latex to the

The author's finished carpet bag (1989, 12 in. by 14 in. by 3½ in.) is trimmed in suede and has an antique clasp.

Wearables made from hooked pieces are sewn like other garments, except that a zipper foot is used to allow for stitching closer to the hooked edge.

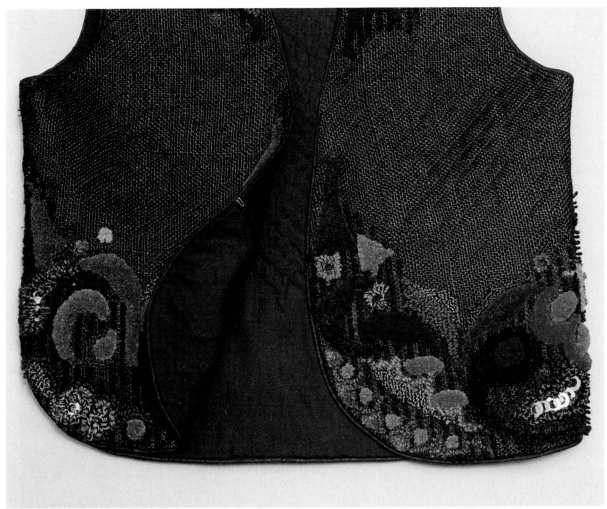

Handworked additions of beads and sewn piping give the finishing touch to wearable garments, as shown here on the author's hooked vest.

backing, working only in the hooked areas. Immediately afterwards, size the seam allowances with a diluted white-glue solution. As with rugs and hangings, the latex secures the hooking to the backing, and the sizing prevents the edges from raveling. Leave the latexed work on the frame to dry overnight.

When the pieces are completely dry, remove them carefully from the frame and cut them out, leaving ⅝-in. to 1-in. seam allowances around each piece. Construct the wearable or accessory using a straight machine stitch with a zipper foot, sewing as close to the hooked area as the needle will allow. If the work is to be lined, cut out a sep-

arate lining shell from the original pattern, and construct and attach the lining in the traditional dressmaking manner.

One of my favorite things about making hooked wearables and accessories is the opportunity they give you to include elegant, whimsical or unique details. Functional additions such as fasteners should be located and attached with care. Other purely decorative embellishments, such as embroidery, beading or small metal elements, can be handled more freely, but these additions could be sewn on by hand, using sturdy thread in a color that will match the hooked area to which they are applied.

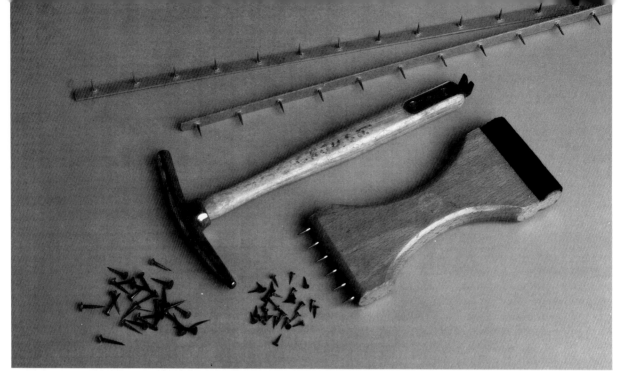

Common tools used for upholstery include (from top, clockwise) upholsterer's cardboard seam tacking, a tack hammer, a webbing stretcher, and small and large upholstery tacks.

Finishing an upholstered rocking-chair seat

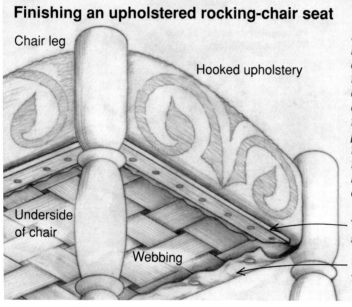

Chair leg

Hooked upholstery

Underside of chair

Webbing

Finishing an upholstered chair seat involves three simple steps. First, carefully position the hooked fabric over the seat cushion and tack it temporarily on all four sides. Second, starting on one side, take out the tacks temporarily, turn under a hem on the backing fabric, pull the fabric tightly over the seat's frame and drive in tacks to secure the fabric permanently. Finally, lightly hammer in place upholsterer's seam tacking centered over the folded hem.

½-in. upholsterer's seam tacking attached to frame to secure backing hem

Nonhooked backing turned under temporarily and tacked

Finishing hooked pieces to be used as upholstery is not very different from finishing rugs, wall hangings and wearables. The piece is clipped, vacuumed and latexed, and the hems are sized. As with garments, make sure to latex only the hooked areas to prevent the seams from becoming too stiff to turn under during upholstery installa-tion. Cut out the hooked piece once it's completely dry, leaving ample seam allowances. If you're experienced at upholstery techniques, apply the hooked work to the furniture, securing with upholstery tacks in traditional methods. If you're a novice upholsterer, take the hooked work to a professional for completion.

Installation

Once you've finished and hemmed your rug or wall hanging, the one remaining step is to install it in its final home. Persevere through this last stage—many works can fall short of their potential if they are not properly installed.

You may think there's nothing to be said about installing a rug, but this isn't true. It's not difficult to install a rug, but care must be taken to ensure that the work will have a long life and to prevent damage to any carpet or flooring beneath it. Consider the traffic patterns through the area when laying the rug down. If the rug will be walked up-on—and there's no reason it shouldn't be if you've constructed it well and used good materials—set up a regular rotation schedule so that the rug receives even wear.

If the back of your finished rug is rough, you may want to put down a rug pad. This provides more comfort underfoot and protects the rug from wear. A rug pad is especially welcome on rough stone, slate or brick floors. Rubberized rug padding comes in several varieties and densities. I find the heavy foam pads often lift the rug awkwardly high off the floor. Because I like rugs to look fairly flat on the floor, I use the plastic-coated grid style of pad instead. Check with a carpet store for types of padding available in your area.

A rubberized pad in a grid pattern protects the rug and floor without adding bulk. The turned-back edge on this rug reveals two types of hem treatments: a simple hem (running vertically in the picture) made from the open weave of the backing and an applied canvas-backed hem (running horizontally). Because of the different hemming fabrics, a simple overlapped corner was used instead of a miter.

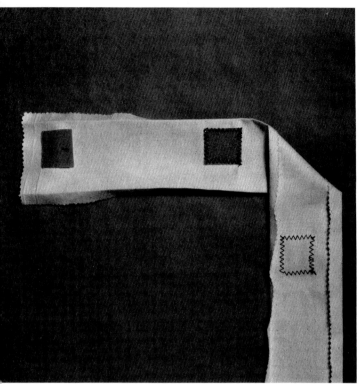

Installing wall works

Even though a work may have been designed for the floor, you may decide to hang it on the wall. Whether the piece was originally intended for wall or floor, the approach to installing it on the wall is the same. Wall-hanging installation is made simple with the use of Velcro interlocking tape (see p. 94 for more on Velcro).

I hope the person who invented Velcro knows what a blessing it's been for fiber enthusiasts. I know of no other installation technique that can compare in terms of simplicity and ease of use. Velcro gives professional results, even in the hands of novices. I use nothing else, even for hanging art rugs on the wall.

To apply Velcro for installing a piece, sew the soft half to the hem of the hooked piece and apply the matching stiff band to a wood support (see the drawing below), which will be attached to the wall. The Velcro is never sewn through the hooked area of the finished work. For wall hangings 3 ft. square or less, use ¾-in. wide Velcro, cut in 1½-in. to 2-in. long pieces. Sew the tape onto the hem (not through the hooked surface) at 6-in. intervals, with a straight or zigzag machine stitch. For heavier and larger wall hangings over 3 ft. square, stitch 1½-in. or 2-in. wide Velcro, cut in lengths 1½ in. long. Sew the Velcro pieces on the top hem, spacing them about 6 in. apart. You'll find that Velcro is such a tenacious and effective material that even short lengths are strong enough

An easy and effective way to hang hooked wall works is to use Velcro. To eliminate the awkwardness of handling a bulky finished piece, Velcro can be attached first to a canvas hem, and then the hem is stitched to the top back edge of the finished wall piece. Shown at the left of the hemming strip is a Velcro piece pinned and ready to be sewn. At right are two other pieces, shown from front and back, already stitched to the canvas strip.

Flat mount

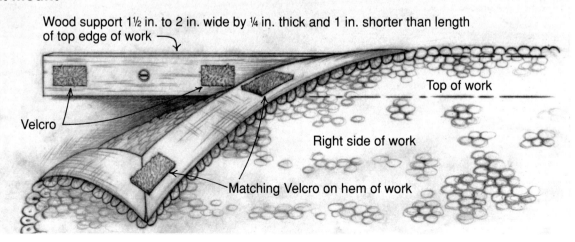

Wood support 1½ in. to 2 in. wide by ¼ in. thick and 1 in. shorter than length of top edge of work

Velcro

Top of work

Right side of work

Matching Velcro on hem of work

Flat mount for a multi-part work

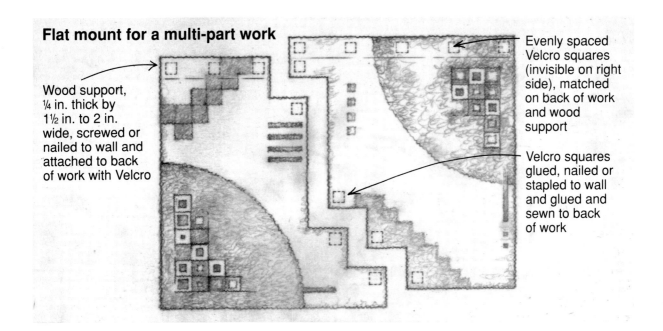

Wood support,
¼ in. thick by
1½ in. to 2 in.
wide, screwed or
nailed to wall and
attached to back
of work with Velcro

Evenly spaced
Velcro squares
(invisible on right
side), matched
on back of work
and wood
support

Velcro squares
glued, nailed or
stapled to wall
and glued and
sewn to back
of work

to hold very heavy hooked pieces. Large or continuous strips are unnecessary as well as costly.

There are three different points during the hooking process (discussed below) when you can attach the Velcro to the hooked piece. To find which works best for your particular piece, study the work and where you want it to be hung. Think through the various steps in making the piece and decide at which point it makes most sense to attach the Velcro. Remember that the soft Velcro parts are sewn on the hooked piece, and the matching stiff Velcro is attached to the wood support. Once you've applied the Velcro, follow the hemming instructions suggested.

You can sew Velcro on at the very beginning of your hooking project, even before the backing has been stretched onto the frame. This is the ideal method if you know exactly what the finished size of the work will be. Measure evenly spaced strips, and sew the soft Velcro parts onto the hem of the top side.

Another option is to sew the Velcro pieces on after the hooking is completed and removed from the frame, but before the work is hemmed. Attach the Velcro pieces with machine stitching across the hem of the top side. If the wall hanging is large or particularly heavy, however, this approach can be difficult. You may find that you need an assistant to help hold and maneuver this bulk through the sewing machine.

To avoid struggling with detailed stitching on the entire work at the sewing machine, it's sometimes easier to sew pieces of Velcro on a separate strip of fabric first. This strip is then sewn to the hem with straight machine stitching before it is turned under.

After the Velcro is attached and the hanging is hemmed and finished, it's time to make the matching wall support. This wood strip will have the stiff half of the Velcro applied to it and will be securely mounted to the wall. When the Velcro on the wall support is matched up with the Velcro on the finished work, the piece will hang securely.

For a flat installation, in which the piece hangs flat against the wall, use a wood support ¼ in. thick by 1½ in. to 2 in. wide. The wood support will be 1 in. shorter than the top edge of the finished work, so that none of the mounting shows once the work is hung. If you're installing a multipart piece whose sections you want positioned slightly apart, each section will need its own wood support (see the drawing above).

The flat mount can be varied to produce a floating installation, in which the work extends a few inches away from the wall. This installation gives the work a dimensional look, as if it were floating

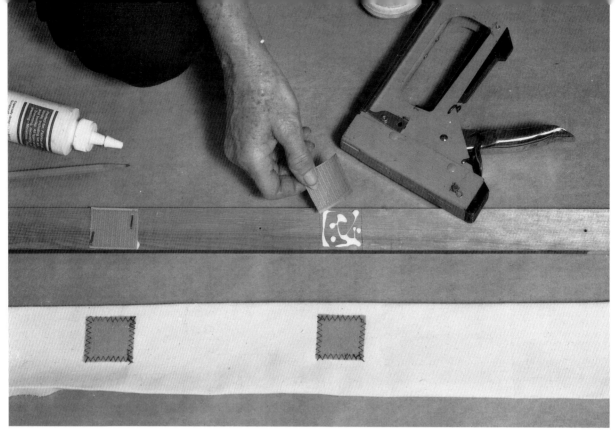

Care must be taken to align the two halves of the Velcro on the hem of the work and the wood support that will attach the work to the wall. The Velcro for the wood strip is attached initially with adhesive, then secured permanently with two staples.

Floating mount

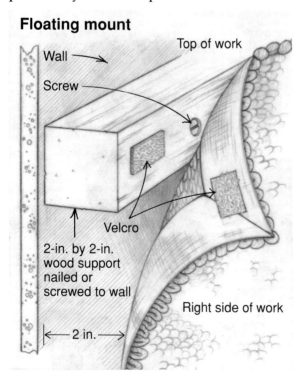

Wall

Top of work

Screw

Velcro

2-in. by 2-in. wood support nailed or screwed to wall

Right side of work

← 2 in. →

freely in space (see the drawing at left). For a floating installation, use a 2x2 wood support that's an inch shorter than the top edge of the finished hanging. (For larger pieces, you might need to use a thicker wood support, but still keep it an inch shorter than the width of the finished work.).

The most important part of the installation process is making accurate measurements when spacing the Velcro pieces on the hanging and the wooden support so that they eventually line up. Once the Velcro has been attached to the finished fiber piece, apply the Velcro pieces to the wood support. Working on a flat surface like a table or floor, lay the finished work flat, right side up. Place the wood support beneath the top edge of the work, centering the wood so it doesn't show—usually it will be positioned about ½ in. in from the top and sides of this edge.

Using the Velcro pieces on the finished work as a guide, mark the wood exactly where the matching stiff Velcro strips are to go, using a pencil or marking pen. Then remove the wood support and glue the Velcro pieces in position with Tacky Glue

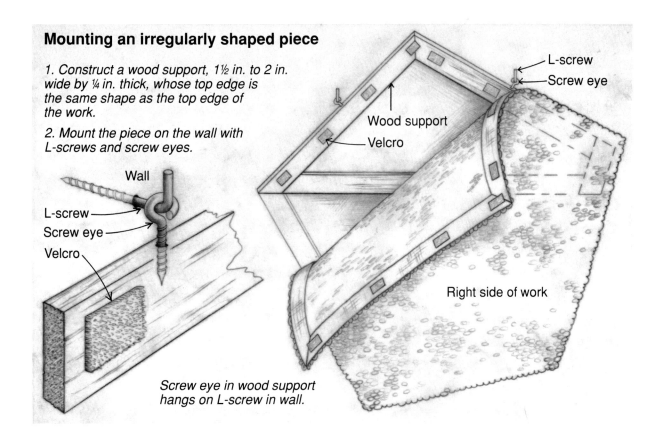

Mounting an irregularly shaped piece

1. Construct a wood support, 1½ in. to 2 in. wide by ¼ in. thick, whose top edge is the same shape as the top edge of the work.

2. Mount the piece on the wall with L-screws and screw eyes.

L-screw
Screw eye
Wood support
Velcro
Wall
L-screw
Screw eye
Velcro
Right side of work

Screw eye in wood support hangs on L-screw in wall.

or Super Tacky adhesive. To reinforce the bond, use a staple gun to secure the Velcro to the wood support with two staples. Place weights on the glued and stapled Velcro pieces and allow them to dry overnight.

For irregularly shaped hooked works, the same principle of supports applies (see the drawing above), except that more pieces of wood are necessary to fit the top of the wall hanging. The important step is to determine which edges of the finished work require support so that the work will lie flat against the surface of the wall. Simply holding the piece up will show you the points where support is needed. Each work will create different demands, but, generally speaking, the support points are along the topmost edge.

Fit and measure the wood supports either by using the paper cartoon as a guide or by laying the hanging flat. As with the other mountings, each support should be placed ½ in. from the top and side edges so the wood will not show when the work is installed.

If the work will be moved from time to time, it's wise to label the wood supports as well as the back of the fiber piece itself with directional markings like top, left and right. Once the support pieces have been taken off the wall and handled a few times, it's easy to get the parts confused. A simple marking system will save you a lot of time and trouble.

When you are ready to hang the wood support on the wall, drill small holes in the wood where the nails or screws will go, using a drill bit slightly smaller than the shank of the nail or screw. Predrilling will prevent the wood from splitting during the installation process. Another method of attaching the support to the wall is to place two small screw eyes on the narrow top edge of the wood, spaced evenly from each end. The wood support can then be attached to the wall by hammering a nail through the opening in each screw eye or by slipping the screw eyes over the end of thin L-shaped screw hooks that you mounted into the wall.

Once the adhesive has dried, the wood strip is fastened to the wall and the fiber piece hung by pressing together the matching Velcro halves. If the work is to be moved, both fiber and wood pieces should be clearly marked with directional labels to avoid confusion in subsequent hanging.

Once you've attached the wooden support to the wall, hang the fiber work by matching the Velcro squares. Beginning at one end and working across the top to the other end, press the Velcro halves together until there is a secure bond. Once most of the weight of the work is on the wall, final adjustments can be made easily by pulling the Velcro areas apart and rejoining the work and the mounting support in precise alignment.

Care and cleaning

I believe that more fiber works are ruined by improper cleaning than by soil itself. Because most handmade articles are more fragile than manufactured objects, they must be treated differently. The vigorous brush of a vacuum cleaner can in no time destroy a beautiful work that should last a lifetime. And too often the cleaning products sold to remove stains and dirt actually set these stains for life. We have been tricked into thinking that a commercial bottle of magic will work better than our own common sense. After spending months making these rugs, I'm committed to taking care of them to keep them in the best condition.

The best way to approach dirt and stain removal is to take steps to keep the piece clean to begin with. Consider carefully where you hang or place your finished works. I rarely put my rugs in a place where they'll need more than a regular vacuuming. You won't find any of these laboriously hand-hooked rugs at my kitchen door for muddy feet to wipe upon, or in any other well-trafficked areas. They deserve the respect that any work of art demands. If placed under coffee tables, dining tables or conversation areas away from central traffic zones, these rugs will remain beautiful and bring you enjoyment for many years.

Fiber is very absorbent; it will pick up not only liquid but also smoke and other airborne particles. To ward off stains and dirt, I use a spray-on soil retardant like Scotchgard. Spray several light applications on the finished work. When the solution is dry, test it with a drop of water. If the fiber absorbs the water, the seal has not been made completely, and more spray is needed. Soil retardants work best on cottons and smooth materials. Porous wools may require several light applications.

Another necessary protection for woolen pieces is mothproofing. Although most commercial wools are permanently mothproofed these days, hand-spun wools and commercial wools of older stock are not. Any wools not mothproofed can be treated by running the yarns and fabrics through a "do-it-yourself" dry cleaner before they are hooked. An unusual way to mothproof your yarns and fibers is by placing them in the freezer, which will kill the moth larvae.

There are several methods of cleaning hooked works, depending on the type of stain and the extent of the dirt. Manual methods like vacuuming or shaking are most common, or you can send pieces out for professional dry cleaning. Localized spots and stains should be cleaned as soon as possible after they've occurred.

Vacuuming is the best general method of cleaning hooked works. Try to vacuum before dirt has become embedded in the work, and make sure never to use a brush-action vacuum cleaner. That powerful, furiously revolving brush can whip any textured and fragile surface to fuzz in minutes. A canister or tank-type vacuum with good suction has become one of my primary tools. It's not only by my side while I'm hooking and clipping, but it also makes quick work of dirt removal. By using just the air suction with the upholstery attachment or the nozzle alone, the dust and dirt can be removed without destroying any fibers. If a piece has delicate fibers, never let the attachment touch the fibers. Always use the least amount of agitating action possible. Let the air suction do the work and don't be concerned — the latex backing will hold the fibers securely.

Textile conservators often protect a flat work during cleaning by holding a piece of plastic screening between the vacuum and the work (see the photo above right). The screening prevents any fragile fibers from being sucked into the vacuum hose. If you're not using the screening, hold your hand over any long loops or fragile fibers to keep them from being sucked up into the nozzle.

Shaking hooked works or hanging them outdoors is another good method of cleaning. A good airing outdoors and an occasional fluffing of the pile can keep pieces looking fresh and eliminate odors or other embedded particles.

When dealing with liquid stains, most permanent damage can be prevented if the stain is removed immediately with absorbent paper or terrycloth toweling. For rugs, place several layers of toweling over the stain, and step firmly on the toweling to wick the moisture from the fiber into the towel. You may have to use a lot of towels and repeat this process if the stain is big or very wet. If any discoloration remains, sponge the area with cold water, taking care not to overscrub or get the rug too wet. If the stain persists, try a solution of

To protect delicate fibers from the strong suction of a vacuum hose during cleaning, hold a piece of plastic screening over the fiber. Dirt and dust pass through the mesh, while the threads are protected from damage.

white vinegar or household ammonia (either one diluted with cool water). Don't use soap or detergent to spot-clean, since it's too difficult to rinse and remove the suds completely. Once the stain disappears, blot all excess moisture with clean toweling, brush the nap up lightly by hand and allow it to dry completely.

Solid-food stains are best removed by carefully lifting the food off the piece immediately so as not to force the matter deeper into the fiber. It may be better to use a knife or a spatula than a sponge, to avoid rubbing the stain into the fiber.

I haven't yet found a commercial rug cleaner I like. They all seem to soak the soil into, not out of, the fiber. I prefer to wash the piece by hand if the materials are all colorfast and the work is not too large. This is particularly effective for heavily soiled rugs or more durable pieces. But keep in mind that a wet rug can become extremely heavy. When washing cottons and synthetics, it's best to use warm water, while wools prefer a cool wash with special cold-water liquid detergents.

To wash a rug, use a large bathtub filled with water and a mild liquid detergent. Submerge the rug in water, keeping it as flat as possible. Press down gently on the rug, then move over a few inches and press down gently again. Continue "kneading" the rug, working over its entire surface to force the water to saturate the fiber completely. Do not scrub or twist. Allow the rug to soak for several minutes, then gently knead it again. Without removing the rug from the tub, drain the water and refill the tub with clean water and more detergent. Repeat this entire operation until the water is no longer dirty.

Rinse the rug until the water runs clear. Drain the tub, then hang the work right side up on a strong rod like a broom handle placed over the tub. When most of the water has drained out of the rug, remove it from the tub and hang it evenly over a sturdy metal or wooden rod away from direct sunlight. Allow the work to drip dry for several days without squeezing or wringing it.

If you decide to dry-clean your work, select a reputable dry-cleaning firm, if possible one that specializes in Oriental or specialty rugs. Give them as much information as possible regarding the fiber content, how the piece was made, what dyes were used, whether the fiber is colorfast and any other useful construction details. If a latex backing was used, ordinary dry-cleaning solvents will dissolve or weaken it, and you may have to make an additional application of latex when you retrieve the work from the cleaners. Usually a few loops or ends of fibers will have worked their way past the surface, making it necessary to clip these ends to maintain the original look. For smaller unlatexed pieces, it's often safer to clean them at the "do-it-yourself" dry-cleaning store rather than to send them to a careless dry cleaner.

Once the works have been cleaned, you may want to store them. For temporary storage, I hang the pieces over smooth rods right side up (textured side out) with plastic sheeting draped on top to protect them. When storing or shipping works in boxes, I like to fold the highly textured pieces, layering them with plenty of bubble wrap. Many people prefer to roll their hooked works right side out, but I find that my method of folding and layering with bubble wrap crushes the fibers less. If you're storing the works in boxes for long periods, they should be placed in acid-free cartons with acid-free tissue generously layered between the folds to prevent fiber from touching fiber. With any storage, be sure to protect the work from exposure to extreme temperatures (both high and low) as well as excessive humidity, which would cause the fiber to mildew or rot.

Repairing hooked work

No matter how careful you are with your scissors during the hooking process, you can expect to snip through the backing material occasionally. Any cut must be taken care of at once to prevent further breakage or raveling. If only one or two threads are cut, a small dab of diluted white-glue

If you inadvertently cut the backing material, repair the area at once to prevent further raveling or damage. To repair slight damage from clipped threads, apply a dab of diluted white-glue solution to the cut area. Let it dry thoroughly, then gently hook over the area.

Repairing cut backing

Reweave backing, following over-and-under weave. Apply diluted white glue to strengthen repair, if necessary.

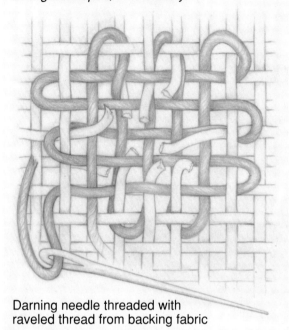

Darning needle threaded with raveled thread from backing fabric

solution applied with the tip of a brush is usually enough to bind the threads together and repair the area. Don't attempt to hook in or around the repaired area until the adhesive is completely dry, or you'll open up the cut even more and do greater damage. When the area is dry, hook with caution to fill the weakened area. Add a light wash of adhesive over this area when it's hooked if further strengthening is necessary.

If several threads are cut, actual reweaving or darning will be necessary. Brush a very diluted white-glue solution carefully over the cut, extending about ½ in. around each edge to stabilize the weave. Once the area has dried completely, ravel a thread from the edge of the backing material to use as darning material. With a darning needle, reweave the area, stitching in and out, over and under, and following the same open weave as the backing. Continue working up and down the grid pattern until the cut is closed. When the darning is complete, add a light wash of adhesive to hold the

repair. Let the repaired area dry completely before you resume hooking.

Repairs may also have to be made to the hooked area itself. If a work is damaged after the piece is finished, you may have to make repairs with new material. After completing a work, I usually put together a sampling of yarns, cut yardage and other materials that were used in the work. I save these, along with my original sketches and patterns, in a plastic bag, away from dust and light. In the event that a work needs to be repaired with new materials, I can immediately pull out the collection of original materials used in the piece, without having to scramble and figure out exactly what I incorporated into the work when I made it. Extra springs or other unusual elements can also be stored in the bag so that you can replace them quickly and easily. If you keep a watchful eye for damage and make small repairs as they are needed, your work should last for many years.

Long before I ever finish a piece, I'm mentally planning the next one—choosing colors, thinking of unusual materials to try and new techniques to use. Each project provides the creative step for the one to follow, and it's this evolving nature of hooked work that I so enjoy. Each piece carries the thrill of some special discovery, whether it be a new fiber, an unusual process or some fresh mix of color and texture. With so many new ideas and textures to explore, I'm always eagerly awaiting the next fresh canvas and the chance to begin the process all over again.

LAKE LEELANAU

5

A Gallery of Contemporary Hooked Work

Within the past few years, rug hooking has enjoyed a tremendous surge in popularity. Now the medium of choice for many fiber artists, rug hooking today serves to capture both traditional and very contemporary imagery. From realistic landscape to impressionistic portrait, from painterly abstract to sheer whimsy, the hooked canvas today has numerous and varied faces. A sampling of this broad spectrum of contemporary hooked work is shown on these and the following pages.

Martha Opdahl, Greencastle, Indiana. At right:
Alex's Xes; **1986; 99 in. by 73 in.; tufted wool, cotton backing. (Photo by Pierson Photographics.) Below:** *Winter Lattice;* **1988; 96 in. by 72 in.; tufted wool, cotton backing. (Photo by Gary Chillufo.)**

■ "My work is an effort to present felt tensions as visual tensions. The tensions represent my desire to be spontaneous, impulsive, energetic and even reckless, and an equally compelling need for control, restraint and order. Visually, dynamic elements interact with controlling structures.

"I find that more and more I want to challenge these orderly structures and work on the brink of disruption, baiting chaos. I seek a simultaneity of order and disorder, holding out against equilibrium. I try to show what life feels like, yet create a work with a life of its own."

—*Martha Opdahl*

Roslyn Logsdon, Laurel, Maryland. Above: *Daytona Beach;* **1980; 25 in. by 38 in.; wool on burlap. At right:** *Hotel St. Louis II;* **1986; 27 in. by 18½ in.; wool on burlap.**

■ "The two kinds of images I work with are people and buildings. In both, I am concerned with relationships: relationships between people, whether they are a group of friends at the shore or a crowd; and relationships between architectural elements such as windows, shutters, and doors or facades of stone, brick and wood. My urban scenes are more concerned with pattern, while my people are more intimate and are meant to be part of everyone's history."

— Roslyn Logsdon

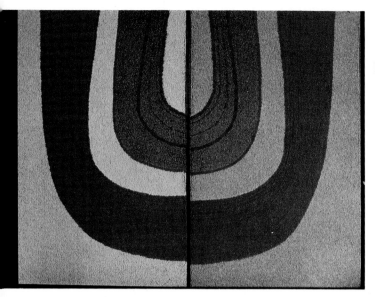

Hildegarde Klene, Herndon, Virginia. Untitled (diptych); 1983; 72 in. by 84 in.; commercial and hand-dyed wool.

■ Klene uses a punch needle in all her hooking because of the control and versatility it offers. A large percentage of the wool yarns, which she uses exclusively for their low sheen, is dyed in her studio. Many of her large-scale works are for corporate and institutional installations.

Pam Smith-Bell, Suttons Bay, Michigan. *Mickey's Toys;* **1988; 36 in. by 48 in.; hand-dyed wool.**

■ This rug was commissioned as a birthday gift to Mickey Gordon, a collector of old tin wind-up toys, by his wife. She took pictures of 14 of his favorite toys and sent them to the artist to incorporate into the rug. The name on the rug refers to the owner, not to Mickey Mouse, as the mice in the rug predate Walt Disney.

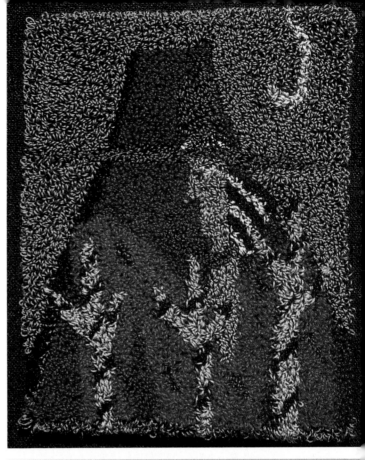

Connie Lehman, Elizabeth, Colorado. Top: *carla longs for ruby mt.;* 1986; 4¼ in. by 3¾ in.; igolochkoy on silk. Bottom: *skinny boy bruce;* 1988; 5 in. by 4¼ in.; igolochkoy on silk.

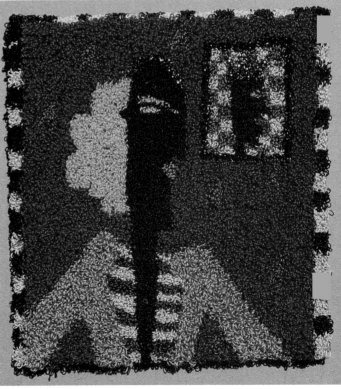

■ "The technique I use for my work is called igolochkoy, or Russian needlepunch. It is done on silk noil with Metler Swiss cotton, silk or Balger metallic thread (usually a combination). It is an obscure technique originally used by Old Believers in Russia, and was used to decorate their bright clothing."

Lehman explains her introduction to igolochkoy: "I saw a small sample in a weaving shop and bought the needle, took it home and spent the summer finding the best fabrics and threads to use."

—*Connie Lehman*

Carol Prine, Arlington, Texas; *The Llama Tapestry;* **1988; 48 in. by 36 in.; wool strips hooked on burlap.**

■The artist and her husband raise llamas on their Texas ranch and spin, weave and process the fleece for fiber projects.

Maggie McLea, Glastonbury, Connecticut. *Serenity: Castles on the Rhine;* **1988; 12 in. by 16 in.; needlepoint and hooking.**

Judith West, Greensboro, North Carolina. *Windfall;*
1986; 35 in. by 52 in.; locker hooking and shirring of
fabric on rug canvas.

■ This piece was created at a time when the artist was
undergoing numerous changes—among them a
new job and the birth of her first son—and just
beginning to work with personal imagery. The
pyramid represents home permanence and security;
the red circles, apples and traditional American
values; and the stairs, the road to security.

Linda Eyerman, St. Louis, Missouri. *Cole County*
Nexus; 1985; 48 in. by 156 in.; hooked wall panel.

■ "I extol the notion of labor-intensive handicraft
as virtue....The process itself becomes a kind of
subtext to the particular image, icon or written
message that the viewer sees and understands
as the finished product."

—*Linda Eyerman*

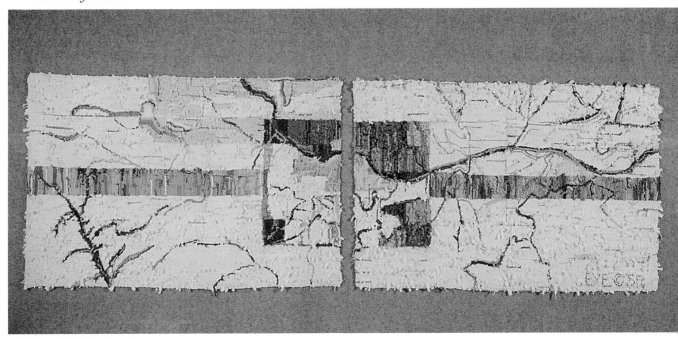

D. Marie Bresch, Carson City, Nevada. *Tulip Splendor;* 1985; 38 in. by 22 in.; wool strips.

■ "This work was hooked in the traditional manner, using wool strips in the primitive technique of minimal shading, but the modern lines of the work change primitive to contemporary."

— *D. Marie Bresch*

Ferrilyn Sourdiffe for Preston McAdoo Rugs, North Bennington, Vermont. *Holsteins;* 1985; 36 in. by 53 in.; wool.

■ McAdoo Rugs is a cottage industry of hand-hooked rugmaking started in 1975 by the McAdoo family. The rugs are designed by members of the McAdoo family and produced in a 200-year-old mill in North Bennington, Vermont. The firm also employs several home-based craftsmen in the area, including many Laotian refugees, who have been taught to hook by Preston McAdoo.

Carrie Jacobson, Capitola, California.
Hummingbird Rug; **1988; 84 in. by 108 in.; wool and rayon.**

■ This custom-designed rug features examples of 14 hummingbirds whose range covers the western United States south to Central America. The artist used 63 different color combinations of wool and 7 colors of rayon yarn to capture the iridescence and delicacy of the birds.

George Wells Rugs, Inc., Glen Head, New York.
Vegetable Oblong; **1987; 32 in. by 55 in.; hand-dyed wools.**

Arlyn Ende, Bradyville, Tennessee. At right: *Footwork: In the Spirit of Scott Joplin;* **1986; 72 in. by 52 in.; wool and fabrics in hooked variations. (Collection, Tandy Rice, Nashville.) Below:** *Gardens of Tyco Brahe;* **1986; 48 in. by 72 in.; wool in hooked variations. (Photos by Gary Dryden.)**

■ In speaking about her shift from creating large wall textiles to work underfoot, Ende comments: "I am not usually conscious of the creative process at work, but when this perception dawned, I felt suddenly freed from the frontality of the wall, and what had been a neutral plane beneath my feet became an exciting, earth-connected design surface.

"I admit to still being ambivalent about having my work walked on..., but I know that art underfoot can have an equal impact to art on the wall."

—*Arlyn Ende*

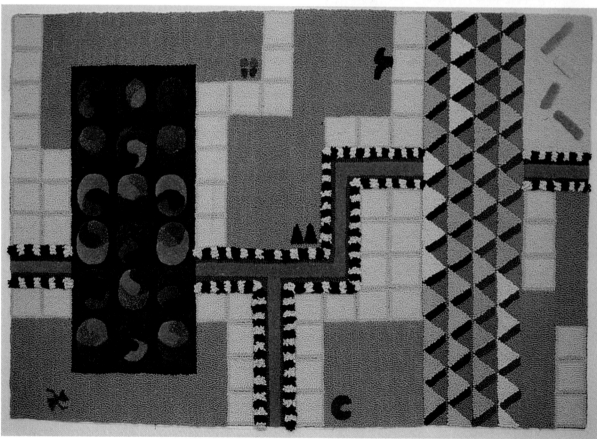

Joan Moshimer, Kennebunkport, Maine. *Sailors' Homecoming;* **1985; 59 in. in diameter; hand-dyed wools.
(Photo by Robert Moshimer, courtesy of** *Rug Hooking* **Magazine.)**

■Moshimer explains that many of her pieces are inspired by the seacoast, where she has lived for the
past 40 years. This piece, worked traditionally, was designed as a gift for a friend.

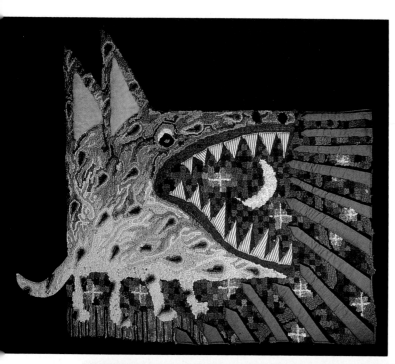

John L. Skau, Greensboro, North Carolina. At left: *Fido;* 1987; 59 in. by 71 in; locker hooking and appliqué on rug canvas. Below: *Flip Side;* 1989; 42 in. by 68 in.; machine tufting, embroidery and appliqué with fabrics and thread on rug canvas.

■ Skau attributes the imagery in the piece at left to a dog that jumped his fence one afternoon when he was outside with his baby. After the incident, all he could remember of the dog was the size of its teeth.

Patti Handley, Fresno, California.
Early Green; **1989; 92 in. by 56 in.;**
wool. (Collection of Wild,
Carter, Tipton & Oliver,
Fresno, California.)

■ Handley thinks of her work as "painting in yarn" and has discovered that she can "do more things with fiber than with paint, in terms of richness, warmth, texture and depth of color."

Resources

As rug-hooking enthusiasts, you'll develop your own favorite sources of equipment, supplies and materials. Just as important are information resources — books, information, organizations — to keep you informed and inspired. The following list is brief and intended to start you on your own search for favorite resources. When contacting these firms and organizations, you may wish to include a self-addressed stamped envelope (SASE) for a speedier reply.

Supplies

Aardvark Adventures
P. O. Box 2449
Livermore, CA 94551-0241
(415) 443-2687
Metallics, beads, threads, paints, supplies. Quarterly catalog, $2.00.

A/E Textiles
Route 1, Box 25
Bradyville, TN 37026
Frame loom with unique L-shaped design. Write for information and prices.

Bartlettyarns, Inc.
P.O. Box 36GC
Harmony, ME 04942-0036
(207) 683-2251 or 2341
Wool yarns spun in Maine.

Braid-Aid
466 Washington Street
Pembroke, MA 02359
(617) 826-6091
Wool, cutters, rug backings and foundations. Catalog, $4.00.

Century House Rug Hooking Studio
562 Pembroke Street West
Pembroke, Ontario K8A 5P3
Canada
(613) 732-9744
Silk-screened patterns for traditional rug hooking.

Cerulean Blue, Ltd.
P.O. Box 21168
Seattle, WA 98111-3168
(206) 443-7744
Supplies, books. Catalog, $4.50.

Gloria E. Crouse
4325 John Luhr Road, N.E.
Olympia, WA 98506
(206) 491-1980
Supply kits, needles, backing, adhesive; workshops. Send SASE for information.

Davidson's Old Mill Yarn
P.O. Box 8
Eaton Rapids, MI 48827
(517) 663-2711
Wool rug yarns, mill ends.

The Dorr Mill Store
P.O. Box 88
Guild, NH 03754
(603) 863-1197
Wool yardage, burlap.

The Fiber Studio
Foster Hill Road, P.O. Box 637
Henniker, NH 03242
(603) 428-7830
Yarns. Samples, $3.00

Frederick J. Fawcett, Inc.
1304 Scott Street
Petaluma, CA 94954
(707) 762-3362
Linens.

Forestheart Studio
21 South Carroll Street
Frederick, MD 21701
(301) 695-4815
Linen backing material, dyes, cutters, frames, wool, hooks.

George Wells Rugs, Inc.
565 Cedar Swamp Road
Glen Head, NY 11545
(516) 676-2056
Punch needle, wool, supplies.

Gleaners Yarn Barn
Highway 5, North, P.O. Box 1191
Canton, GA 30114
(404) 479-5083
Wool rug yarns.

Halcyon Yarn
12 School Street
Bath, ME 04530
(207) 442-7909; (800) 341-0282

Harry M. Fraser Co.
R. & R. Machine Co., Inc.
192 Hartford Road
Manchester, CT 06040
(203) 649-2304
Supplies, cutters.

Herrschners'
Hoover Road
Stevens Point, WI 54492
(715) 341-4554
Strip-It cloth stripper, punch needle, supplies.

Joan Moshimer's Rug Hooker
Studio
Box 351
Kennebunkport, ME 04046
(207) 967-3711
Supplies. Catalog, $6.00.

Mandy's Wool Shed
Route 1, P.O. Box 2680
Litchfield, ME 04350
(207) 582-5059
Wool yardage.

Paternayan
445 Main Street
West Townsend, MA 01474
(508) 597-8794, (800) 225-6340
Wool yarns.

J. D. Paulsen
P. O. Box 158
Bridgton, ME 04009
Rigby cloth stripper.

Rittermere-Hurst-Field
45 Tyler Street, Box 487
Aurora, Ontario L4G 3L6
Canada; (416) 841-1616
**Designs, supplies. Catalog,
$6.00, prepaid.**

Robin & Russ Handweavers
533 North Adams Street
McMinnville, OR 97128
(503) 472-5760
Yarns.

Rumpelstiltskin's
Route 1, Box 915
Hillsboro, OR 97124
(503) 629-2174
Electric and hand needles.

Ruth Ann's Wool
R. D. 4, Box 340
Muncy, PA 17756
(717) 546-5548
**100% wool yardage, supplies.
Color card, $2.00.**

Whispering Hill Farm
Box 186, Route 169
South Woodstock, CT 06267
(203) 928-0162
Supplies.

Books

Books can instruct as well as
inspire. In addition to the brief
listing below, check the design
and craft section in your local
library or bookstore as well as
general books on art and design.

Albers, Anni. *On Designing.*
Middletown, Conn.: Wesleyan
University Press, 1962.

Blumenthal, Betsy, and Kathryn
Kreider. *Hands on Dyeing.*
Loveland, Colo.: Interweave
Press, 1988.

Cuyler, Susanna. *The High-Pile
Rug Book.* New York: Harper &
Row, 1974.

Dale, Julie S. *Art to Wear.* New
York: Abbeville Press, 1986.

Fassett, Kaffe. *Glorious
Needlepoint.* New York: Crown
Publishers, 1987.

Fiberarts Design Book and
Fiberarts Design Book Two.
Edited by Fiberarts Magazine.
Fiberarts Design Book Three.
Edited by Kate Mathews.
Asheville, N.C.: Lark Books,
1980, 1983 and 1987, respectively.

Itten, Johannes. *The Art of
Color.* New York: Van Nostrand
Reinhold, 1974.

_____. *Elements of
Color.* Ed., Faber Birren. New
York: Van Nostrand Reinhold,
1970.

Kent, William Winthrop. *The
Hooked Rug.* Reprint of 1941 ed.
Detroit: Gale Research, 1971.

Knutson, Linda. *Synthetic Dyes
for Natural Fibers.* Loveland,
Colo.: Interweave Press, 1986.

Kopp, Joel, and Kate Kopp.
*American Hooked and Sewn
Rugs.* New York: E. P. Dutton &
Co., 1975.

Lambert, Patricia, Barbara
Staepelaere and Mary G. Fry.ß
Color and Fiber. West Chester,
Pa.: Schiffer, 1986.

Larsen, Jack Lenor, and Alfred
Buhler. *The Dyer's Art.* New
York: Van Nostrand Reinhold,
1977.

Larsen, Jack Lenor, and Mildred
Constantine. *The Art Fabric:
Mainstream.* New York:
Kodansha, 1986.

_____. *Beyond
Craft: The Art Fabric.* New
York: Kodansha, 1986.

McRae, Bobbi. *The Fabric &
Fiber Sourcebook.* Newtown,
Conn.: The Taunton Press, 1989.

Parker, Xenia Ley. *Hooked Rugs
& Ryas.* Chicago: Henry
Regnery, 1973.

Porcella, Yvonne. *A Colorful
Book.* Modesto, Calif.: Porcella
Studios, 1986.

Stocksdale, Joy. *Polychromatic Screen Printing*. Berkeley, Calif.: Oregon Street Press, 1984.

Stockton, James. *Designer's Guide to Color*. San Francisco: Chronicle Books, 1984.

Sutton, Ann. *The Structure of Weaving*. Asheville, N.C.: Lark Books, 1983.

Wiseman, Ann. *Rag Tapestries and Wool Mosaics*. New York: Van Nostrand Reinhold, 1969.

Zarbock, Barbara J. *The Complete Book of Rug Hooking*. New York: Van Nostrand Reinhold, 1969.

Znamierowski, Nell. *Step by Step Rugmaking*. New York: Golden Press, 1972.

Magazines

The fiber and craft magazines listed here offer a current view of the field and its activities. Other general publications often contain articles on rug hooking.

American Craft
American Craft Council
40 West 53rd Street
New York, NY 10019

Color Trends
Michele Wipplinger
8037 9th N.W.
Seattle, WA 98117

Crafts
Crafts Council
1 Oxendon Street
London, SW1Y 4AT
England

The Crafts Report Publishing Co., Inc.
700 Orange Street
P.O. Box 1992
Wilmington, DE 19899

Fiberarts
Nine Press
50 College Street
Asheville, NC 28801

The Flying Needle
National Standards Council of American Embroiderers
588 St. Charles Avenue, N. E.
Atlanta, GA 30308

Handwoven
Interweave Press
306 North Washington Avenue
Loveland, CO 80537

Rug Hooking
Commonwealth Communication Services, Inc.
P.O. Box 15760
Harrisburg, PA 17105

Shuttle, Spindle & Dyepot
Handweavers Guild of America
120 Mountain Avenue, B101
Bloomfield, CT 06002

Surface Design Journal
Surface Design Newsletter
Surface Design Association
4111 Lincoln Boulevard, #426
Marina del Rey, CA 90292

Threads magazine
The Taunton Press
63 South Main Street
P.O. Box 5506
Newtown, CT 06470-5506

Organizations

Fiber and craft organizations give you the opportunity to share information and stay in touch with other rug-hooking enthusiasts. Many of the following national organizations have regional chapters. There are also many statewide designer/craft organizations with active fiber memberships.

American Craft Council
40 West 53rd Street
New York, NY 10019

Association of Traditional Hooking Artists (ATHA)
c/o B. J. Andreas
50 Cape Florida Drive
Key Biscayne, FL 33149

The Embroiderers' Guild of America
335 West Broadway, Suite 100
Louisville, KY 40202

Handweavers Guild of America
120 Mountain Avenue, B101
Bloomfield, CT 06002

National Standards Council of American Embroiderers
P. O. Box 8578
Northfield, IL 60093-8578

Surface Design Association
4111 Lincoln Boulevard, #426
Marina del Rey, CA 90292

Index

Editor: Terri Lonier
Senior editor: Christine Timmons
Designer: Deborah Fillion
Layout artist: Cathy Cassidy
Illustrator: Pat Schories
Art/production manager: Robert Olah
Copy editor: Peter Chapman
Production editor: Ruth Dobsevage
Editorial assistant: Maria Angione
Art assistants: Jodie Delohery, Iliana Koehler
Computer-applications specialist: Margot Knorr
Print production manager: Peggy Dutton
Indexer: Harriet Hodges

Typeface: Palatino
Paper: Warrenflo, 70 lb., neutral pH
Printer and binder: Ringier America
                    New Berlin, Wisconsin